SEEN AND FELT
Around Town
by Linean Soyt

★ Actress Hermitus Minnor stars in *Resurrection* Extravaganza Calvary Theater. Sold out house for six years.

★ Mayor Hyball reveals plan to exterminate enemies with poison beer and pretzels.

★ Socialite Morry Dool undergoes finger extension surgery. Expects full recovery.

★ Artist Toto Turno begins underwater color painting on Endil River basin. Crowds line both shores to see results.

★ Philanthropist Morris Azore gives one million dollars to corner hot-dog vendor with stipulation that he not provide sauerkraut.

★ Man–about-town Herman Beinnor forsakes shoelaces in attempt to change image. Plunges to death off city curb.

★ Prima–donna Leyla Gizzar wins acclaim in new production of "My Only Chance" - an operetta based

...on her failed marriage to Socialite Morry Dool.

★ Veal Magnate Horace Kotler leans against kitchen wall and causes...

Socialite Morry Dool

★ One-time poster-boy Melus Sandro is publically humiliated at Dept. of Sanitation.

★ Comedy star Nonny Rapture learns to smear inner TV screen with vaseline during live broadcast... viewers ransom.

★ Pet-food magnate Namish save... poodle feces... secret can...

★ Sex-god... es million... secret. To... rance.

★ Cigar... Berzilof... President... perspirat...

TOP CAS...
UNUSUA...
INFORM...

REMEMBER:
While you slept NOTHING HAPPENED!

UPPER TOOTH PULLED BUT ROOT REMAINS
3:21 A.M., Loosevelt Hospital. In a miraculous case of compulsive regeneration, Herve Gezzel, had a molar extracted only to discover that the root of the tooth was still in place and exuding a sweet, cotton-candy flavor.

Mystery Sentence Spoken Before Assembly

Man Compelled to Read Newspaper Continuously
12:21 P.M., Cungula Ave. George Zilltile found himself unable and unwilling to stop reading the newspaper. In one day, he went through a week's papers, reading non-stop through meals, baths and on... He was unable to sleep for... falling behind in his reading.

An abnormal interest in details of each advertisement, article of minor importance enabled Mr. Zilltile to fill... the consumption of ne...

...gpajamas. I need a practical course! I can't start in the middle with a class full of students half my age!"

11:21 P.M., lobby Hotel Lully, white woman, aged 28 in street clothes: "Please stop and say you'll help me move my (indecipherable word here). I have a beautiful room on the 28th floor, but I need your help, please!"

11:45 P.M., Ganzer Street Delicatessen, child in arms of father: "Can't we wait until mama comes home for dinner? Let's play with the television. I'm not tired."

11:53 P.M., corner Ganzer and Holveet, hispanic male, age 48: "Oh brother, stop the buses. Oh brother, stop the buses. Con medda esquerville bus."

12:01 A.M., Holveet Ave. bus, rear, white male age 68: "They're no good to me whatsoever! No good. That's all. I don't want discuss it any further. They're just no good. I wanna get my money back."

12:12 A.M., Gondola Donut Shop. Black male, age 54 in pajamas: "I wanna roast beef sandwich. I'm putting in my order now for tomorrow afternoon. Roast beef on white bread, lettuce and tomato. Nothing to drink."

12:18 A.M., lobby Vitascope Theater, white male age 73 in shirt only: "Is this place air-conditioned? Jesus Christ, I'm dying from the heat. Where's my wife? Who turned the bed around? (wakes here)."

Same Dream in Two People
2:06 A.M., Kissel Ave. Two, socially and biologically unrelated individuals: Maria Ulock and Louis Polp, had the identical dream last night.

Both dreamt that they were unjustly sentenced to be boiled alive in a cauldron of vegetable soup and both were spared by the unpleasant flavor of their tears.

A Lifetime Lived in 2 Minutes!
Rapidity of Thought in Sleep Astonishes Experts!
12:21 A.M., Kestral Nursing Home. In a two-minute period of sleep, nursing home patient, ...lpeust, experienced a lifetime's worth ...hip and pleasure, work and leisure, ...d companionship.

...h details of a complete life: accident of ...nily background, education, employ-...rriage, retirement and death, were described by the elderly woman to an attendant on the night-shift and subsequently reported to a staff psychologist.

In no way did this imagined life coincide with Mrs. Gollpeust's actual life experiences. Mrs. Gollpeust had no first-hand knowledge of...

UNBORN CHILD APPEARS AS LUNCHEONETTE SPECIAL
3:16 A.M., Poluka Apts. The image of an naked, unborn baby appeared on the counter of Sanzor's Luncheonette last Christmas Eve. The bachelor, Norman Ahvell, had refused to order the child even though it was offered as the "daily special" and at a reduced price.

Mr. Ahvell had obstinately ordered a tuna fish sandwich instead. When...

...was overwhelmed by a terrible feeling of guilt.

Onlookers were disgusted by Mr. Ahvell's selfish behavior; other patrons had order the "special," why didn't he? At the end of the day, the kitchen would be left with dozen of unsold, unwanted, and unborn children.

Mr. Ahvell left the luncheonette,...

...Refreshments were offered after the speech, but no one partook of them.

...Curiously, his comp... national and world affairs remained on the level of a four-year-old child.

♩ DATE DUE

REAL ESTATE PHOTOGRAPHER
Stories
by Ben Katchor

Introduction by Michael Chabon

LB
1837

Little, Brown and Company
New York Boston

curb detail

REAR
WINDOW
VIEW

NO-INCOM...
APARTM...

NOTE: View...
second story
window of
cafeteria
entrance

For Susie Taube

THANKS TO:
Jem Cohen, Edmund Leites,
Bob Milgrom, Martin Schwartz,
Mark Stokes, Alexander Theroux,
Tobi Tobias, Lawrence Weschler,
Dave Wool; Jonathan Rosen &
Robin Cembalest of the Forward;
Dave Isay, Cindy Carpien,
Scott Simon, Caryl Wheeler,

Henry Sapoznik and the cast
of The Knipl Radio-Cartoons:
Jerry Stiller, Joey Faye,
"Professor" Irwin Corey,
Brother Theodore, Bob Fass,
Eddie Lawrence and Sally DeMay
ALSO
THE GUGGENHEIM
MEMORIAL FOUNDATION
for its generous support.

POST CARD

THIS SIDE IS FOR THE ADDRESS

Cafefare City at Dusk, View from Garden of Eden
Cafeteria. Photo by Dalliance Studios.
8746?.

Genuine Man-Made Colors · The Gratitude Co., Hyena, NY

ELEVATED TRAC...

CIGAR STORE

CAFETERIA

STOP #...

A PRELIMINARY STUDY OF LIGHT
AND SHADOW ...
...EMENT. THIS IS
...RRORS IN
ONLY!

Cigarette Butt
Receptacle

EL...
...HADOW

...FTER RAIN SHOWER

1:20 POLYCHROME

SELLADORE & ASSOC.

Copyright © 1996 by Ben Katchor
Introduction copyright © 1996 by Michael Chabon

All rights reserved. No part of this book may be reproduced in any
form or by any electronic or mechanical means, including information
storage and retrieval systems, without permission in writing from the
publisher, except by a reviewer who may quote brief passages in a
review.

Little, Brown and Company
Time Warner Book Group
1271 Avenue of the Americas, New York, NY 10020
Visit our Web site at www.twbookmark.com

First Edition

The characters and events in this book are fictitious. Any similarity to
real persons, living or dead, is coincidental and not intended by the
author.

ISBN 0-316-48294-3
Library of Congress Catalog Card Number 96-26580

10 9 8 7 6

SC

Manufactured in China

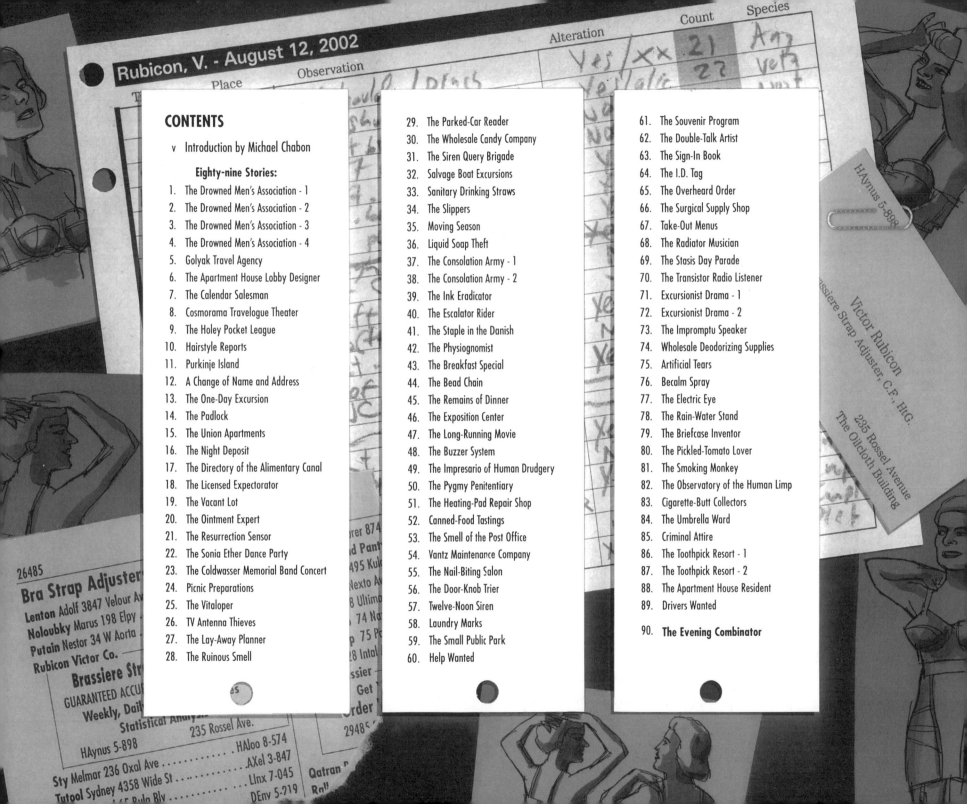

CONTENTS

May 19, 1957 — **The Public Directory of The Alimentary Canal**

Eads, W., 35 Posht . . . . Gastritis, Abdomin. Cramps, Sluggish Bowels
Eadston, F, 274 Acra . . . Fecal Impact., Diverticulitis, hemorrhoids
Eager, A., 89 Hemp . . . . Diarrhea, Irritable colon, Rectal Fissure
Eagle, M., 104 Moly . . . . . Aerophagy, Colitis, Sluggish bowel
Eaglet, T., 37 Samson . . . . Proactalgia Fugax, Gas, Diarrhea
Eamen, S, 127 Tymp. . . . . . Aerophagy, Dyspepsia, cramps
Eanut, V., 87 Hyve . . . . Runs, Gas, Violent Wind in the morning
Ebato, L, 109 Lymanol . . Piles, Irritable Colon, Gas, Piles on occassion
Ebayot, K., 90 Stimen . . . Hemorrhoids, Constipation, Vomiting
Ebbis, U., 678 Vynut . . . . . . Diarrhea, Duodenitis, Incipient Hemorrhoids
Ebcony, W., 87 Intolandi . . . . . . Clear
Ecanatsy, H., 76 Pellit . . . . Violent Gas
Ecolls, Y., 655 Hiunit . . . . Clear
Edenal, S., 87 Fully . . . . Hemorrhoids, Gas, Stomach Ulcer, Heartburn
Edenay, E., 178 Yolla . . . . . Aerophagy, Malodorous Gas, Constipaion
Edgarat, R., 298 Benuta . . . . Clear
Edgona, D., 890 S. Yolk . . . . Sluggish Bowel, Hemorrhoids
Egons, T., 76 Putter . . . Diarrhea, Runs
Egrattis, R., 654 Lonrin . . . . . . Diarrhea
Ehin, G., 87 Mionot . . . . Fecal Impactment, Constipation
Ehipotsky, G., 76 Gogol . Gas, Vomiting
Ehony, K., 543 Belons . . . Hemorrhoids
Ekin, O., 76 Mutanta . . . . . . Gastritis, Cramps
Ekonat, U.,
Ekopula, Y.,
Elonatis, P.,
Emans, U.,
Emonis,

Emmitual, T., 76 Wawal . . Stomach Ulcer, Jaundice, Rectal Fissur
Emmonas, H., 176 Svell . . . . . Peptic Ulc Wind, Biliousness and
Emmonitis, Y., 65 Zore . . . Biliousne Wind, Diarrhea, Anal
Enaboly, G., 542 Pellit . . . . . . Diarrh Rectal Bleeding, Anal fissure ,
Enacana, T., 76 Fully . . . . . . Constipat Piles, Runs in morni
Enadona, G., 938Hyve . . . . . . Fistul Nausea, Vomiting
Enaena, H., 76 Moly . . . . Piles, Violen Gas, Fissures and Crack
Enafry, G., 298 Tymp . . . . .
Enagol, S., 472 Leely . . . Stomac
Enahsky, T., 87 Yondar . . . .
G., 76 Go
543 Belon
264 Putter . . .

Eraline, G., 76 Bully . . . . . . Peptic Piles, Gas T., 76 Fully
Erasmus, B., 76 Binatol . . . . G., 938Hyv Bowels, Hemorrh
Erasula, T., 45 Benuta . . . 76 Moly Impactment, C 98 Tymp

INTRODUCTION

Like many people, I was first apprised of the wistful and intrepid pilgrimage on which you are about to embark by Lawrence Weschler, in his *New Yorker* profile of Ben Katchor, creator of the last great American comic strip.

It is a sad duty thus to anoint *Julius Knipl, Real Estate Photographer.* Perhaps no art form has ever flourished so brilliantly only to decline into such utter debasement, in such a brief period of time, as the newspaper strip. Reading the comics page in 1996, exactly one hundred years after the debut of Outcault's *Yellow Kid*, is, for those who still bother, half melancholy habit and half sentimental adherence to duty, a daily running up of a discredited flag in a forsaken outpost of an empire that collapsed.

Weschler's article dwelt at length, as do most commentators on Katchor, on the artist's preoccupation with the sensuous residuum of the past, those unexpected revelators of the all-but-forgotten, encountered in the stairwell of a hard-luck office building or on the dusty shelves of a decrepit pharmacy, those stray remnants of an earlier time that are hinted at in the surname of his protagonist, the stoop-shouldered wanderer, meditative soul, and former dance instructor Mr. Julius Knipl. And it is true that celebration of the chance survival, the memory wrapped like a *knipl*, or nest egg, in a beaded purse of forgetfulness, discovered in the back of a drawer, is the most immediately striking and perhaps the most accessible aspect of the strip. It was this aspect, initially, that led me to track down Katchor's first collection of strips, *Cheap Novelties*, and—the spell was on me now—to take out a subscription to *Forward*, currently the flagship paper of the scattershot and fluctuating *Knipl* syndicate. I'm a sucker, myself, for such chance survivals, because as I've confessed elsewhere I suffer intensely from bouts, at times almost disabling, of a limitless, all-encompassing nostalgia, extending well back into the years before I was born.

The mass synthesis, marketing, and distribution of versions and simulacrums of an artificial past, perfected over the last thirty years or so, has ruined the reputation and driven a fatal stake through the heart of nostalgia. Those of us who cannot make it from one end of a street to another without being momentarily upended by some fragment of outmoded typography, curve of chrome fender, or whiff of lavender hair oil from the pate of a semi-retired neighbor are compelled by the disrepute into which nostalgia has fallen to mourn secretly the passing of a million marvelous quotidian things.

The erasure of the past, and its replacement by animatronic replicas, politicians' narratives, and the fictions of advertisers, coupled with the explosive proliferation of new inventions and altered mores, ought to have produced a boom time for honest mourners of the vanished. Instead we find ourselves haunting the margins of a world loud with speculators in metal lunch boxes and Barbie dolls, postmodernists, and retro-rockers, quietly regretting the alternate chuckling and sighs of an old-style telephone when you dialed it. We are not, as our critics would claim, necessarily convinced that things were once better than they are now, nor that we ourselves, our parents, or our grandparents were happier "back then." We are simply like those savants in the Borges story who stumble upon certain objects and totems that turn out to be the random emanations and proofs of the existence of Tlön. The past is another planet; anyone ought to wonder, as we do, at any traces of it that turn up in this.

Every week, in the eight panels of a new installment of *Julius Knipl, Real Estate Photographer*, Ben Katchor manages to teleport the reader to a particular urban past—a crumbling, lunar cityscape of brick and wire that was young and raucous in the heyday of the Yellow Kid. It's a world of rumpled suits, fireproof office blocks with the date of their erection engraved on the pediment, transom windows, and hare-brained if ingenious small businesses; a sleepless, hacking-cough, dyspeptic, masculine world the color of the stained lining of a hat. (This world, in its dreamlike, at times almost Dadaistic particulars, may not ever, precisely, have existed; and yet a walk through the remaining grimy, unrenovated, simulacrum-free streets of any old American downtown, with their medical-supply showrooms, flophouses, theosophical book depositories, and 99¢ stores, can be a remarkably persuasive argument for the documentary force of Katchor's work.)

But Katchor is more—far more—than a simple archaeologist of outmoded technologies and abandoned pastimes. In fact he often plays a kind of involuted Borgesian game with the entire notion of nostalgia itself, proving that one can feel nostalgia not only for times before one's own but, surprisingly, for things that never existed. Not content with or perhaps, in this age of debased nostalgia, too rigorous an artist to evoke merely the factual elements of a vanished past so easily appropriated by admen and Republican candidates, Katchor carefully devises a seemingly endless series of regrets, in the heart of Julius Knipl, for things not only gone or rapidly disappearing, such as paper straws and television aerials, but also wholly imaginary: the Vitaloper, the Directory of the Alimentary Canal, tapeworm sanctuaries, a once-well-known brand of aerosol tranquilizer.

As, over the weeks, I joined Mr. Knipl in his peregrinations, I discovered, as will you, that the strip's wonderful evocation of an entirely plausible and heartbreaking if only partly veracious past is not the greatest of its pleasures or achievements. Ben Katchor is an extremely clever, skillful, and amusing storyteller.

With the exception of mute (and to me dreadfully tedious) strips such as *Henry* and *The Little King*, the comic strip is and has always been a literary form that braids words and pictures, inextricably, into a story. In the so-called Golden Age of the comic strip, standards with regard to both elements were often high; lately the pictures have dwindled to a bare series of thumbnail sketches, and while the notion of story has atrophied almost to nonexistence, most of the burden of humor or pathos now falls, for better or worse, on the words. But we have never—at least not since Herriman—had a writer like Katchor.

His polished, terse, and versatile prose, capable, in a single sentence strung expertly from a rhythmic frame of captions, of running from graceful elegy to police-blotter declarative to Catskill belly rumble, lays down the bare-bones elements, the newspaper-lead essentials, of his story. As in all great strips, Katchor's dialogue—the hybrid element unique to comics, neither quite picture nor completely words—swelling perilously inside his crooked and deformed balloons, drives, embellishes, shanghais, and comments—generally ironically—on the story, his woebegone characters sometimes echoing the taciturn elegance of the captions, sometimes speaking in an entertaining mishmash of commercial travelers' argot, Lower East Side expostulations, and the sprung accents of cheap melodrama.

None of this would mean anything, however, without Katchor's artwork, running in perpetual counterpoint to and tension with the captions and dialogue. Though his style in no way resembles that of either Jack Kirby or Will Eisner, Ben Katchor is, along with them, one of the three great depictors of New York City in the history of comics (Katchor's city, nameless or whatever its name may be, is always, plainly, New York). It is a dark, at times almost submarine city, with antecedents in sources as divergent as the work of Hopper, de Chirico, and Ditko. Wide, deserted streets find themselves hemmed in on all sides by carefully-not-quite-anonymous buildings. Late-night cafeterias extrude wan panels of light onto the sidewalks. Lonely newsvendors stand beside dolmens of unsold papers.

Katchor's style, like all the great styles, is addictive. His wobbly lines, woozy perspectives, and restless shifts in point of view; his intense exploitation of a narrow spectrum of ink washes running from soot to dirty rain; his use of detail at once lavish and superbly economical, painstaking and apt; his lumbering, sad, paunchy, hollow-eyed, jowly, blue-jawed men in their ill-fitting suits; his rare, mildly frightening women in their remarkable armor of trusses and lingerie—none of it is beautiful, or even, if I may be forgiven for saying so, masterly; the same could have been said about Herriman. In the funny papers a mastery of the vocabulary of comic drawing is

more important than refinement of technique. Drawing skill matters only insofar as it helps the cartoonist to tell his story.

The stories Katchor tells, mostly in eight or nine panels on a single page, occasionally spilling over onto two, three, or four pages (and, wondrously, in the case of the longest and previously unpublished story in this collection, onto seventeen wild pages with an astonishing splash panel), fall, roughly, into seven categories.

There are, first of all, the famous requiems for vanished places, sale items, novelties, and devices. There are episodes and accounts which serve to illuminate the ways and behaviors, from the Stasis Day Parade to the hazardous umbrella situation to the intricacies of Excursionist Drama, of the alternate Gotham in which Mr. Knipl makes his living. There are anecdotes and incidents taken from the lore of the local tradesmen, its hairstyle mappers, licensed expectorators, parked-car readers, and numerous cracked inventors. There are the odd, indirect, at times almost eventless stories so like dreams—the dreams beloved of readers of *The Evening Combinator*—that they linger and disturb. There are stories, inevitably but somehow incidentally, of Mr. Knipl himself, a lonely man in a city of lonely men, and stories of some of those other *solitaires:* Emmanuel Chirrup, Arthur Mammal, Carmine Delaps, Al Mooner.

In the end it isn't nostalgia but loneliness, of an impossible beauty

and profundity, that is the great theme of *Knipl*. Katchor's city is a city of men who live alone in small apartments, tormented by memories, impracticable plans, stains on the ceiling. Small wonder, then, that they should so eagerly band together, over and over again, into the fantastic and prodigious array of clubs, brotherhoods, retirement communities, and secret societies, accounts of which make up the seventh category of *Knipl* story. "Fellowship," as a loyal member of the Holey Pocket League tells Mr. Knipl, "is the only thing we crave."

All seven of these typical narratives converge in "The Evening Combinator," through whose seventeen pages Katchor begins, not without regret presumably, to effect an evacuation from the blasted country of the newspaper strip to the rumored paradise of something known, a hundred years after a bald boy in a yellow nightdress first appeared in the lonely, teeming streets of New York City, as the graphic story. Interesting things are happening there; whether they ever reach the level of high quality combined with mass readership of the great comic strips—the creation of immense shared hallucinations—remains to be seen. Perhaps in a broken, nocturnal, past-haunted city of solitary wanderers and lunatic leagues, like this one, such universal fantasies, and the fellowship they provide, are no longer possible. No matter how we crave them.

—**Michael Chabon**

THE FRUIT OF AN ORCHARD TRANSFORMED INTO A PAN OF BAKED APPLES ON A CAFETERIA STEAM TABLE.

THE SCENT OF A MIMOSA TREE

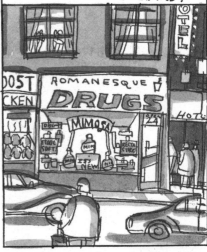

PRESERVED IN ALCOHOL AND OFFERED FOR SALE IN AN ALL-NIGHT DRUG STORE ON ROMAN BOULEVARD.

THE SOUND OF KATYDIDS

RECORDED AND PIPED THROUGH THE HALLWAYS AND LOBBY OF A MID-TOWN APARTMENT HOUSE AT NIGHT.

MR. KNIPL DONATES TWENTY-FIVE CENTS TOWARD THE UPKEEP OF A RURAL ASYLUM ESTABLISHED BY 'THE DROWNED MEN'S ASSOCIATION.'

HERE, THIS LOOKS GOOD.

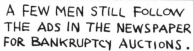

A FEW MEN STILL FOLLOW THE ADS IN THE NEWSPAPER FOR BANKRUPTCY AUCTIONS.

TSIMTSUM INDUSTRIES, INC. MONDAY MORNING 10 A.M.

THEY RECOGNIZE THE OLD, FAMILIAR NAMES, THE UNSOLD INVENTORIES

10,000 ARTIFICIAL LEATHER PHYLACTERIES, 5,000 POLYESTER PRAYER SHAWLS, PLUS ASSORTED NOVELTY MEZUZOTH.

AND THE CONTENTS OF A FORSAKEN OFFICE.

I BET THEY DIDN'T EVEN EMPTY THE WASTEPAPER BASKETS.

THEY FEEL THE URGE TO RUN BACK TO THE CITY AND PUT IN A BID,

IF I LEAVE TONIGHT, I CAN SLEEP OVER AT MY DAUGHTER'S PLACE AND THEN TAKE A CAB IN THE MORNING.

TO PROFIT FROM SOMEONE ELSE'S FAILURE,

I'M TELLING YOU... NOBODY'LL BE THERE.

BUT THEN THE EVENING BUS ARRIVES

GOOD RIDDANCE HOTEL

AND THE DINING ROOM OPENS FOR THE FIRST SITTING.

I WAS A SALESMAN WITH TSIMTSUM.

AT FIVE O'CLOCK EACH EVENING, A BUS WAITS ON THE CORNER OF ROMAN BOULEVARD AND ROSSEL AVENUE

TO SAVE THOSE MEN WHO HAVE GONE UNDER FOR THE THIRD TIME.

THE MONEY JOHNNY SUMAC WOULD HAVE EARNED THE NEXT DAY BY CONVINCING PEOPLE TO BUY A NEW KITCHEN TABLE WILL, INSTEAD, REMAIN IN THEIR POCKETS.

A SMALL PORTION OF THIS MOMENTARY SURPLUS WILL BE DONATED, IN DIMES AND QUARTERS, TO A GOOD CAUSE:

THE MAINTENANCE AND IMPROVEMENT OF THE DROWNED MEN'S ASSOCIATION HOME.

THE PALTRY EXPENDITURES THAT WOULD HAVE BEEN MADE THE NEXT DAY BY JOHNNY SUMAC AND HIS FELLOW RESIDENTS

ARE MORE THAN EQUALLED BY THE ASSOCIATION'S DAILY PURCHASES OF FOOD AND MATERIAL.

BY LEAVING THE CITY FOR THIS RURAL ASYLUM, THESE POOR MEN HAVE, IN FACT, WAIVED THEIR PREROGATIVE TO MAKE MONEY IN EXCHANGE FOR THE BARE NECESSITIES OF LIFE ON A DAILY BASIS.

HE PRIDED HIMSELF ON HAVING NEVER SEEN A LIVE COW

AND YET HAD A PROFOUND UNDERSTANDING OF POT CHEESE IN ALL OF ITS VARIETIES.

A MEDIUM CURD, EXTRA TANGY.

AFTER SIXTEEN YEARS, HIS DESIRE TO MAKE MONEY SUDDENLY WENT DRY, LIKE THE RUBBER GASKET ON AN OLD REFRIGERATOR DOOR.

I JUST CAME BY TO SAY HELLO.

BY CASUALLY POSING SAD LITTLE QUESTIONS OVER THE YEARS,

WHAT IF I WERE CALLED OUT OF TOWN FOR A FEW YEARS?

HE HAD, LIKE ANY OTHER RESPONSIBLE HUSBAND, BEGUN TO PREPARE HIS WIFE AND CHILDREN TO ACCEPT THE IDEA OF HIS EVENTUAL ABSENCE

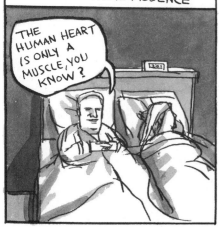

THE HUMAN HEART IS ONLY A MUSCLE, YOU KNOW?

—BUT NOT FOR THIS.

HIS CO-WORKERS SEEMED TO UNDERSTAND.

THE INSTINCT TO SURVIVE IS PERISHABLE. IT ALSO HAS AN EXPIRATION DATE

CARBON COPIES OF EVERY ORDER HE TOOK, A DENSELY PACKED ROLODEX, SCRAPS OF PAPER FILLED WITH PROMISING LEADS AND A MAP OF HIS TERRITORY WERE PLACED ON PUBLIC DISPLAY FOR TWENTY-FOUR HOURS.

A MAN IN A DISTANT CITY WILL STOP AND REMARK, TO HIMSELF,

GOLYAK? GOLYAK?

UPON THE NAME IMPRINTED ON A TOURIST'S SHOULDER BAG

GOLYAK TRAVEL

AND THEN, THAT NIGHT, ALONE IN A STRANGE HOTEL ROOM,

IT'S NOT CLEAR...

TRY DESPERATELY TO RECALL THE SIMPLE WHITE LETTERS

GULYIK... COLJAK... GOLYAK!

WHICH SHED A COMFORTING LIGHT OF REASON OVER THE VICISSITUDES AND DANGERS OF TRAVEL.

BUT BREAKFAST MUST BE INCLUDED.

GOLYAK

THE REPUTATION OF ONE TRAVEL AGENT IS THUS BORNE, ON THE SHOULDER OF AN IDLE TRAVELER,

HOW ABOUT 10 DAYS, 7 NIGHTS IN TBILISI?

WHAT ELSE?

FAR BEYOND THE CONFINES OF A CRAMPED DOWNTOWN OFFICE.

A BACHELOR'S TOUR OF SMYRNA?

ANYTHING ELSE?

HERE! TWO WEEKS LOST IN YAKUTSK!

GOLYAK TRAVEL

UPON BEING HIRED TO RE-DO AN APARTMENT HOUSE LOBBY,

I HAVE A FEW IDEAS.

ALL VISITORS MUST BE ANNOUNCED

ONE INTERIOR DECORATOR FINDS HIMSELF TORN BETWEEN THE PREVAILING STYLISTIC INFLUENCES OF THE DAY.

THE MEN'S ROOM OF AN ART DECO MOVIE THEATER.

A COMBINATION OF TWO OR MORE MOTIFS IS DEEMED NECESSARY TO PRODUCE THE STRONG AESTHETIC AROUSAL

THE DAY NURSERY ON A SOVIET COLLECTIVE FARM.

EXPECTED BY A RESIDENT WHO MAKES THE TRANSITION, TWICE DAILY, FROM DIRTY STREET TO MISÉRABLE APARTMENT.

A LAS VEGAS CASINO

A JAPANESE ROCK GARDEN IN THE RAIN.

THE INTERIOR OF A 19th-CENTURY POWER-HOUSE.

A HALL IN THE GRAND TRIANON AT VERSAILLES.

RING

IN THE END, COST IS THE DECIDING FACTOR.

I CAN GET YOU 150 POUNDS OF WHITE GRAVEL AND SOME RUBBER PLANTS FOR ALMOST NOTHING.

CHIASMA ROCK AND GRAVEL COMPANY

162

BY THE SECOND WEEK OF FEBRUARY OR LINCOLN'S BIRTHDAY,

THAT'S IT. FINISHED FOR THE SEASON.

THE CITY'S WHOLESALE CALENDAR SALESMEN PACK UP THEIR SAMPLES AND ENTER A STATE OF SELF-INDUCED HIBERNATION.

NOW LET THE CHRISTMAS-DECORATION SALESMEN KNOCK THEMSELVES OUT.

THEY REDUCE THEIR WARDROBE TO ONE WOOLEN SUIT AND PUT EVERYTHING ELSE IN MOTH-BALLS.

THEY SLEEP LATE AND, FOR A FEW WEEKS, LUXURIATE IN THE PASSAGE OF UNMARKED TIME.

NOW I'M HUNGRY

ON THE PROWL FOR SUPPER, THEY'LL MEET THEIR PRODUCT (A CUSTOM IMPRINTED GIVEAWAY WITH A DIFFERENT SCENE FOR EACH MONTH OF THE YEAR) AT EVERY TURN.

HUNG ON A STRANGE WALL IT IS EMBARRASSINGLY SMALL AND HOMELY.

AN UNSPOKEN FEAR OF THE PAST SIX MONTHS

CAN THE HOLE IN THIS CALENDAR BEAR THE WEIGHT OF 365 DAYS?

SEEMS NOW, WITH THE COMING OF ST. VALENTINE'S DAY, TO HAVE BEEN FOOLISH AND GROUNDED ON NAUGHT.

IN THE BROKEN VELOUR SEATS OF A TRAVELOGUE THEATER

SUKKOR IS A COMPARATIVELY MODERN CITY POSSESSING BROAD ROADS, GOOD RESIDENTIAL QUARTERS, CONVENIENT SHOPPING AREAS AND EXCELLENT TRANSPORT...

A BUSINESSMAN CAN USUALLY ESCAPE THE HARDSHIPS OF A WEEKDAY MORNING—

YET SOMEWHERE IN THE BACK, A GENTLEMAN WEEPS.

NATURE HAS ENDOWED IT WITH A BRIGHT, SUNNY LOOK AND A FAIRLY COOL CLIMATE

WHOoo... WHOoo...

THROUGH THE CEASELESS NARRATION HE CAN RECOGNIZE THE STREETS AND MONUMENTS OF HIS NATIVE CITY.

THERE IS NO EXTORTIONIST TENDENCY AS EVERY KIND OF MERCHANDISE CAN BE HAD IN ABUNDANCE.

WHOooo... WHOooo... WAH

QUIET!

ALTHOUGH IT IS ONLY ELEVEN O'CLOCK IN THE MORNING, IT IS TOO LATE FOR HIM TO RETRIEVE THE LOST POSSIBILITIES OF HIS YOUTH.

...CROWDED WITH TRAFFIC COMPLICATED BY EIGHTEEN DIFFERENT TYPES OF REGISTERED VEHICLE...

HUT...HUT HUT..HUT

FOR GOD'S SAKE!

HE MOANS THE NAME OF A STREET, A GIRL, OR PERHAPS A CAFÉ TO WHICH HE CAN NEVER RETURN.

...THE LARGEST BISCUIT FACTORY ON THE SUB-CONTINENT

SAPHENA SAPHENA

QUIET!

AN USHER ESCORTS HIM INTO THE LOBBY,

...A SHRINE SURROUNDED BY A MOAT HOUSING TAME CROCODILES...

PLEASE... PLEASE... COME WITH ME.

WHERE THE MANAGER POLITELY EXPLAINS THAT HE IS NOT RUNNING A FUNERAL PARLOR.

YOU'RE AN INTELLIGENT MAN... YOU UNDERSTAND

THE SHORT FILM ENDS SOON AFTER.

IN THE COURSE OF THEIR WORLDLY PURSUITS

IT WILL SUDDENLY COME AS A REVELATION TO A CHOSEN NUMBER OF MEN AND WOMEN.

—LESS FREQUENTLY TO WOMEN, IT IS SAID, BECAUSE THEY CARRY HANDBAGS—

THAT A CONTINUUM EXISTS BETWEEN THEIR POCKET AND THE STREET.

THIS REVELATION IS OFTEN PRECEDED BY A GUST OF COOL AIR UP THE LEG AND THE RING OF A COIN STRIKING THE PAVEMENT.

FROM THAT MOMENT ON, THEIR SENSE OF OWNERSHIP AND PERMANENCE IS RADICALLY ALTERED.

KEYS, COINS AND HARD CANDIES COME AND GO WITHOUT THE INTERVENTION OF THE SELF.

THEY SEE THEMSELVES AS BEING MERELY A WARM CONDUIT BETWEEN THE U.S. MINT AND THE ETERNAL GUTTER.

THERE GOES A CAR EQUIPPED TO RECEIVE THE RADIO COMMANDS

OF A MAN WHO NOW STAYS IN BED

WITH A TEN-YEAR-OLD YELLOW PAGES,

A MAP OF THE CITY'S BEAUTY PARLORS AND BARBER SHOPS

AND THAT MORNING'S BEDEWED NEWSPAPER.

HE EARNS A LIVING BY MAPPING THE MIGRATION OF HAIR STYLES THROUGH-OUT THE CITY.

IN THE COURSE OF A DAY, HE WILL INCIDENTALLY USE THE RADIO CAR TO CONFIRM WHAT HE'S READ IN THE PAPER

AND TO FIND OUT WHETHER ANYONE STILL REMEMBERS HIM.

SAFELY ISOLATED FROM THE POPULOUS STREETS OF MID-TOWN BY THE RUSHING WATERS OF A RIVER,

YET VISIBLE FROM THE SHOULDERS OF A TALL MAN,

STAND THE ASSORTED RUINS OF PURKINJE ISLAND:

THE CRUMBLING BENCHES AND MUD-FILLED POOLS OF THE FIRST AMERICAN TAPEWORM SANCTUARY,

THE OVERGROWN AND NEGLECTED MANIKIN BURIAL GROUND,

THE ABANDONED MUNICIPAL SALIVA STORAGE TANKS,

THE RUINS OF AN ASYLUM FOR PRETZEL ADDICTS

AND THE BASE OF A FALLEN MONUMENT TO THE PHYSIOLOGIST WHO IDENTIFIED THOSE TINY REFLECTIONS OF TABLE LAMPS AND INTIMATE FRIENDS WHICH APPEAR ON THE SURFACE OF AN EYE.

FROM THE LOBBY OF A TRANSIENT'S HOTEL THERE FLOWS INTO THE GUTTER A STREAM OF AMNIOTIC FLUID...

PAST AN EMPLOYMENT AGENCY OFFERING UNFAMILIAR, LOW-PAYING JOBS,

SEVEN-LAYER CAKE WORKER-$8K, BALL-POINT PEN STARTERS-$10K, MEASLES GROOM -$7K...

PAST A SALE ON PERMANENTLY SHINED WORK SHOES AND BELTS MONOGRAMMED WITH THE LETTER 'A'

INTO A SEWER OPPOSITE THE ASYUT RESTAURANT.

WHAT DO I KNOW ABOUT STARTING BALL-POINT PENS? I FEEL LIKE A NEW-BORN BABY.

I'M EVEN CHANGING MY NAME TO ABRA... ER... TO SOMETHING ELSE.

ANYWAY, HERE'S THE TWO HUNDRED DOLLARS I OWE YOU AND THE COFFEE'S ON ME.

I HAVEN'T GOT A TELE-PHONE NUMBER OR PERMANENT ADDRESS YET, BUT I CAN ALWAYS GET IN TOUCH WITH YOU.

SURE. SAME NUMBER, SAME ADDRESS, SAME NAME.

A BARGE, CARRYING ALL THE BIRTH CERTIFICATES ISSUED IN THE YEAR 1948, IS TOWED OUT TO SEA.

EVERYONE TAKES ADVANTAGE OF THIS SPECIAL ONE-DAY EXCURSION FARE.

I'M LOOKING FOR WORK.

THE BUS LEAVES AT EIGHT O'CLOCK IN THE MORNING,

ANYTHING IN THE HOTEL LINE.

ARRIVES THREE HOURS LATER AT A SEASIDE RESORT KNOWN FOR ITS FROZEN CUSTARD,

GOOD LUCK.

AND RETURNS THAT EVENING AT EIGHT O'CLOCK.

I DON'T SEE HIM.

HE MUST HAVE FOUND SOMETHING.

YEAH, A SUCCESSION OF KITCHEN JOBS, A TERRIBLE ACCIDENT WITH AN ICE CRUSHER, TOO MUCH DRINKING...

AND THEN, NINE MONTHS LATER, HE'LL TRY TO USE THE RETURN TICKET TO ATTEND HIS BROTHER'S FUNERAL, OR SOMETHING.

IT NEVER LEFT HIS WALLET— IT'S SHRUNKEN AND DISCOLORED.

YOU CAN SPOT THEM RIGHT AWAY... THEY DIDN'T COME FOR THE FRESH AIR.

A LENGTH OF HEAVY CHAIN LOCKED TO THE SIDEWALK GRATING OF A SUPERMARKET'S CELLAR.

ANY LUNATIC WITH A COMBINATION LOCK CAN STAKE A CLAIM.

THE REMAINS OF AN ABANDONED BUSINESS SCHEME INVOLVING...

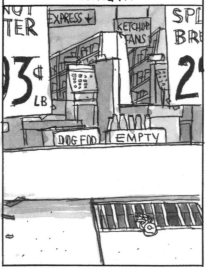

THOSE CANNED GOODS THAT HAVE ACCIDENTALLY LOST THEIR LABELS,

THE ANNUAL CYCLE OF 'SPECIALS,'

THE POOL OF MEN WILLING TO START WORK BEFORE DAYBREAK,

THE POPULARLY ACCEPTED IDEA OF 'MIXED VEGETABLES,'

WE HAVE BROCCOLI, CARROTS OR...

THE AVAILABILITY OF USED HAND TRUCKS

AND A COMBINATION OF NUMBERS AND DIRECTIONS WHICH CAN BE EASILY COMMITTED TO MEMORY.

SIX RIGHT, NINE LEFT, FOUR RIGHT.

ON A CLEAR DAY, MR. KNIPL VISITS HIS FRIEND

NOT MUCH OF A VIEW.

YOU SHOULD HAVE SEEN IT THIRTY YEARS AGO.

ON THE TWELFTH FLOOR OF A HOUSING PROJECT BUILT BY THE AMALGAMATED PANTY-WAIST FITTERS UNION.

WHEN THE MOST INFLUENTIAL MEN IN THE CITY GOT DRESSED EACH MORNING THEY SNAPPED OUR ELASTIC WAIST-BANDS.

IT WAS A POWERFUL UNION, BUT ONCE THE ELASTIC GOES, THE WHOLE GARMENT IS SHOT.

WHEN THE WAIST BAND INDUSTRY LEFT THE CITY, EVERY-THING BEGAN TO DROOP—THE RESTAURANTS, THE THEATER, THE NIGHT-CLUBS...

PEOPLE ARE GOING AROUND SCARED TO TRIP OVER THEIR OWN PANTS.

I REMEMBER WHEN EVERY APARTMENT ON THIS FLOOR HAD A VIEW OF THE HELIX PAJAMA COMPANY, BUT THEY'RE LONG GONE.

I MET MY WIFE THERE.

WHEN SHE WENT INTO THE HOSPITAL FOR THE LAST TIME, AT LEAST SHE KNEW THAT PEOPLE WERE STILL EAGERLY WAITING FOR SOMEONE IN A TWO-BEDROOM TO DIE.

ON A RARE OCCASION, MR. ANGINA WILL ALTER HIS ROUTINE BY CLOSING UP EARLY

AND HIDING THE DAY'S CASH RECEIPTS IN A SECRET INNER POCKET OF HIS PANTS.

TONIGHT, HE MEETS HIS WIFE AT THE THEATER

AND AFTERWARDS DINES AT A FAVORITE RESTAURANT.

AROUND MIDNIGHT, HE TAKES A BICARBONATE OF SODA AND GOES TO BED.

AFTER AN HOUR OF FITFUL SLEEP

HE WAKES AND SEES HIS PANTS, WITH THE BULGING SECRET POCKET, DRAPED OVER A CHAIR

AND GOES TO MAKE A NIGHT DEPOSIT.

ON A SHELF, IN MR. KNIPL'S OFFICE, SITS A SINGLE, DOG-EARED EDITION OF A ONCE-POPULAR REFERENCE WORK—

HELLO, MR. EAGLE, I'M CALLING TO DISCUSS OUR...

"THE PUBLIC DIRECTORY OF THE ALIMENTARY CANAL," IN THIS CASE, FOR THE WEEK OF MAY 19th 1957.

OH, I'M SORRY TO HEAR THAT... NOT FEELING WELL ... I UNDERSTAND ... YOU CAN'T TALK NOW... I'M SORRY.

UPON ITS TISSUE-THIN PAGES, ARRANGED IN ALPHABETICAL ORDER BY FAMILY NAME, ONE COULD SEE AT A GLANCE THE GASTROINTESTINAL CONDITION OF ANY PERSON RESIDING IN THE METROPOLITAN AREA.

CULLED FROM THE MULTITUDE OF REPORTS FILED EACH WEEK BY A VAST, UNDERPAID ARMY OF DRUGSTORE CLERKS, PLUMBER'S ASSISTANTS...

MILTON EAGLE, ONE BOTTLE OF LAXATIVE...

VICTOR EBOMIS, THIRD FLOOR, BACKED-UP TOILET...

DOOR-TO-DOOR CANVASSERS AND PUBLIC-RESTROOM INFORMANTS,

...JUST A FEW QUESTIONS.

THE DIRECTORY'S TWO-LINE SUMMARIES WERE MORE OR LESS ACCURATE.

M. EAGLE, 104 MOLY ST., AEROPHAGY, COLITIS AND SLUGGISH BOWELS.

V. EBOMIS, 87 PAYZEL AVENUE, DIARRHEA, GAS AND CRAMPS.

SHREWD BUSINESSMEN AND SUCCESSFUL SOCIALITES WOULD NOT MAKE A MOVE WITHOUT FIRST CONSULTING THE LATEST EDITION.

HELLO, I'D LIKE TO SPEAK TO MR. EBOMIS.

THEATER OPENINGS AND RESTAURANT PROFITS HINGED UPON ITS AUTHORITATIVE WORD.

OH, CAN'T COME TO THE PHONE RIGHT NOW. YES, I'LL CALL BACK IN FIFTEEN MINUTES.

A MAN STOPS MR. KNIPL IN THE STREET,	SPITS IN HIS FACE	AND THEN HANDS HIM A CARD OF EXPLANATION.	A PASSING POLICEMAN OFFERS HIS SYMPATHY —

YES, THAT'S ME.

"FOR UNDERCUTTING ME ON THE RACHMUNIS JOB. —L. HURON"

I KNOW... IT'S THE LOWEST PROFESSION, BUT PERFECTLY LEGAL... LOOK.

HE POINTS TO A TAG ON THE MAN'S PANTS CUFF.	LATE THAT EVENING, IN A CROWDED CAFETERIA...		HE CROSSES HIS LEGS IN A PARTICULAR WAY SO AS TO AVOID RECOGNITION.

A LICENSED EXPECTORATOR. NOTHING YOU CAN DO BUT HIRE ONE YOURSELF... BUT WHAT'S THE POINT?

Nº738 Licensed Expectorator

EXCUSE ME, IS ANYONE SITTING HERE?

YOU!

ION ERIA GONION CAFETERIA OPEN

OH, HELLO. YES, I REMEMBER ... THE 10 A.M. DELIVERY. PLEASE, HARBOR NO RESENTMENT TOWARD ME, I'M AN UNEMPLOYED SCHOOL TEACHER...

GO ON, YOU CAN HAVE THE TABLE.

IS ANYONE SITTING HERE?

NO, NO, BE MY GUEST.

ON THIS VACANT LOT, CREATED BY THE SUDDEN COLLAPSE OF THE LAPSUS CALAMI CLUB,

THE DEVELOPER, OTTO MANN, ENVISIONS A LAST, GREAT DEPARTMENT STORE.

STARTING WITH BABY SHOES IN THE BASEMENT, WE'LL HAVE A FLOOR DEVOTED TO EACH AGE OF MAN

HIS PARTNER SAYS NOTHING BUT HAS HIS OWN IDEA.

A THIRTY-SEVEN-STORY DENTAL CLINIC WITH A ROOF-TOP BEER GARDEN

AN EMBITTERED ARCHITECT DIGS OUT HIS 1958 PLAN FOR A MIDGET-RACE-CAR TRACK.

NOW THEY'LL BE SORRY!

THE DEPARTMENT OF CIVIL REMORSE PROPOSES A LOVER'S-LANE-TYPE PARK FOR THE SITE.

FOR THE FIRST TIME IN FORTY YEARS, THE SMELL OF AN UNDERGROUND CHEESE-CAKE BAKERY REACHES THE STREET.

AH!

MR. KNIPL IS DRAGGED BY A FRIEND TO SEE THE NEWLY EXPOSED VIEW OF HIS BATHROOM WINDOW,

AND A JUNK DEALER STOPS TO TAKE A LOOK AT WHAT'S ACCUMULATED OVERNIGHT.

AN IMPORTER OF FOLDING RAIN-BONNETS, WITH NO TRAINING IN MEDICINE OR PHARMACOLOGY,

HMM? HERE'S SOMETHING NEW.

HAS, OVER THE YEARS, CONVINCED HIMSELF THAT HE'S ACQUIRED A RARE AND EXTENSIVE KNOWLEDGE OF OINTMENTS AND THEIR EFFECTS ON THE HUMAN BODY.

"DIAPERELLO"...APPLY SPARINGLY TO AFFECTED PART...KEEP CLEAN...

SHOULD ANYONE IN HIS PRESENCE SO MUCH AS MENTION A SKIN DISORDER

IN THE MIDDLE OF THE NIGHT IT STARTS...

OR UNCONSCIOUSLY SCRATCH HIMSELF

A TERRIBLE ITCHING!

A DIAGNOSIS WILL BE OFFERED, FOLLOWED BY AN URGENT PRESCRIPTION FOR THE PRECISE REMEDY, AVAILABLE, OF COURSE, IN OINTMENT FORM OVER THE COUNTER.

IT'S A TYPE OF ECZEMA BROUGHT ON BY NIGHT SWEATS IN AN AIR-CONDITIONED BEDROOM. GET A TUBE OF "POMOLINE-X" IN ANY DRUGSTORE!

CASTING ALL MODESTY ASIDE IN THE NAME OF MEDICAL PROGRESS, HE'LL GO SO FAR AS TO DEMONSTRATE EXACTLY HOW TO APPLY THE STUFF.

...A LITTLE ON THIS FINGER AND THEN YOU REACH OVER... CAREFULLY.

THESE STRANGERS, WHO RARELY CROSS HIS PATH AGAIN,

BECOME, IN HIS MIND, VALUABLE CASE HISTORIES TO BE REFERRED TO AGAIN AND AGAIN AND AGAIN.

...AND THEN THERE WAS A PHOTOGRAPHER WITH ECZEMA ON HIS BUTTOCK!

IN A SHED, ON A HILL OVER-LOOKING A SUBURBAN CEMETERY,

THERE RESTS AN INSTRUMENT CAPABLE OF REGISTERING THE SLIGHTEST PHYSICAL MOTION — THE FIRST SIGN OF A POSSIBLE RESURRECTION!

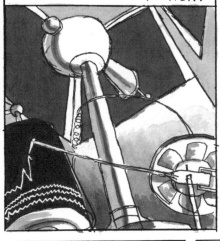

BY MEANS OF A NINETEENTH-CENTURY SYSTEM OF BELL WIRE, THE GLAD TIDINGS ARE RELAYED DIRECTLY TO THE HOME OF A SURVIVING FAMILY MEMBER

AND TO THE CARETAKER'S COTTAGE.

BUT, AS FOREWARNED IN THE CEMETERY'S BROCHURE, NINETY-NINE PER CENT OF ALL ALARMS ARE FALSE.

MUST'VE BEEN A PIGEON

THE DEAD RESUME THEIR SLEEP AND THE INSTRUMENT IS CAREFULLY RESET FOR THE FUTURE.

AN INSTRUMENT SO SENSITIVE IT CAN DETECT A BODY FALLING OUT OF BED WITHIN A TEN-MILE RADIUS.

FROM HERE TO THERE ...TOTALLY BLACK AND BLUE.

THE SAME MEN WHO ESCHEW THEIR NEIGHBORHOOD DANCE SCHOOLS

YOU CAN KEEP YOUR FREE LIFETIME MEMBERSHIP!

WILL RUSH HOME EVERY SUNDAY NIGHT TO WATCH "THE SONIA ETHER DANCE PARTY" ON TV.

SO GLAD YOU COULD MAKE IT TONIGHT.

THE SAME MEN WHO PLAN THEIR VISITS TO THE BASEMENT LAUNDRY ROOM SO AS TO AVOID FEMALE SOCIETY

WILL STUDY WITH GREAT INTEREST THE CREDITS AT THE END OF EACH SHOW.

MISS ETHER'S HATS BY MAX MUCOSA, MISS ETHER'S DRESSES BY PANGOLIN, MISS ETHER'S SHOES BY MESHUMED BROS., MISS ETHER'S STOCKINGS BY FINOULI FINE...

WHILE A GROUP OF MANU-FACTURERS STRIVE TO CREATE THE ILLUSION THAT THE PARTY COULD BE UPSTAIRS,

A MILLION VIEWERS WORK UP A SWEAT EACH SUNDAY NIGHT WITHOUT MOVING A VOLUNTARY MUSCLE.

MONDAY MORNING, THE FOG LIFTS ON A BUSY INTERSTATE HIGHWAY

TO REVEAL A FORTY-FOOT-LONG SMEAR OF MISS ETHER'S FAVORITE SHADE OF LIPSTICK.

ON HIS WAY TO WORK, THE THIRD CLARINET IN THE COLD-WASSER MEMORIAL BAND TRIES TO MENTALLY BALANCE HIS CHECKING ACCOUNT.

GAS $8.39, TELEPHONE $45.92, ELECTRIC $27.24, AND RENT $486.37.

DURING A REST IN THE SIXTH MEASURE OF "THE BLONDZHERER" BY TAKTMAN HE REALIZES THAT HIS JULY RENT CHECK WILL BOUNCE.

DEPOSITS ... $510.00

FOR TEN MONTHS OF THE YEAR, HIS INCOME DERIVES FROM SHORT-TERM SUBSTITUTE JOBS WITH VARIOUS THEATER AND BALLET ORCHESTRAS.

IS PEYSTER STILL IN THE HOSPITAL?

THIS ANNUAL SIX-WEEK ENGAGEMENT IN THE CITY'S PARKS IS THE ONLY STEADY WORK HE KNOWS.

"THE GRAND UNION NOSEBLEED" BY PICKERING

AS THE SUN BEGINS TO SET, THE CHIRPING OF THOUSANDS OF SMALL BIRDS DROWNS OUT THE CLARINET SECTION.

FROM A DISTANCE, NO ONE CAN SEE HIS BROKEN SHOES AND SOILED WHITE SHIRT.

FIFTEEN MINUTES INTO THE NEXT LONG PIECE, "A RADIATOR IN JANUARY" BY PARÉ, THE AUDIENCE BEGINS TO DISPERSE.

WHAT DO YOU EXPECT FOR FREE?

AND THEN, FOR THE CONCERT'S ROUSING FINALE:

"THE SOCIAL SECURITY MARCH" BY KESTIL.

TOMORROW, A FIFTY-PER-CENT CHANCE OF LATE-AFTERNOON SHOWERS...

IN PREPARATION FOR A PICNIC, MR. KNIPL CHOOSES A HILL IN A PUBLIC PARK

WITH A BREEZE, OVERLOOKING THE HARBOR

AND INVITES TWO FRIENDS WHO RARELY EAT IN A RECLINING POSITION.

DON'T WORRY, THE ANTS HAVE NOTHING AGAINST YOU.

THAT NIGHT, HE COMMINGLES THE YOLKS OF EIGHT HARD-BOILED EGGS,

...MOISTEN WITH MAYONNAISE, ADD SALT, PAPRIKA AND A LITTLE DRY MUSTARD.

BUYS SIXTY DOLLARS' WORTH OF COLD-CUTS AND CELERY TONIC

AND WRAPS, IN WAX PAPER, EIGHTY INDIVIDUAL PORTIONS OF SALT AND PEPPER.

IN THE MORNING, THEY SEARCH FOR A CANDY STORE THAT SELLS PAPER KITES.

STOP HERE FOR A MINUTE!

MR. KNIPL FALLS ASLEEP WITH A MUSTARD STAIN ON HIS FOREHEAD.

AND THEN, FOR DESSERT, THE CHILLING TASTE OF AN IMPENDING THUNDERSTORM.

BURIED IN MR. KNIPL'S BASEMENT STORAGE BIN —

A DELUXE MODEL OF AN INGENIOUS EUROPEAN EXERCISE MACHINE FROM THE 1930s.

BROUGHT TO THIS COUNTRY, VIA PARIS, BY AN UNCLE FLEEING FOR HIS LIFE,

IT IS ALL THAT REMAINS OF A NEVER-REALIZED IMPORT BUSINESS.

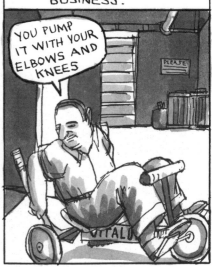

AT SOME POINT, THE UNCLE AWOKE FROM HIS DREAM OF PHYSICAL CULTURE AND WENT TO MAKE A LIVING IN THE DRESS-EMBROIDERY BUSINESS.

TWENTY YEARS LATER, HE DIED OF ARTERIOSCLEROSIS.

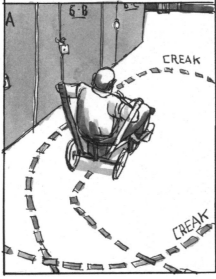

THE SAME MACHINE TURNS UP IN PHOTOGRAPHS OF PRE-WAR BERLIN

LYING UNUSED ON THE AIR-SHAFT PATIOS AND ROOFTOP GARDEN PATHS OF THE LOWER MIDDLE CLASSES.

A GANG OF ENERGETIC BOYS—MORE SCAVENGERS THAN THIEVES—

GATHER ABANDONED TELEVISION ANTENNAS FROM THE ROOFS OF OLD APARTMENT BUILDINGS THAT HAVE BEEN CONVERTED TO CABLE.

THE WORTH OF EACH MODEL, FROM THE HUMBLE "HIGH-AITCH" TO THE MAGNIFICENT "FOUR-COLOR RAINBOW TRACKER,"

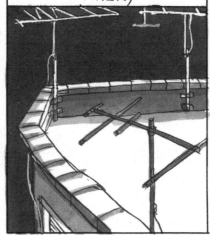

IS NOW REDUCED TO THE CURRENT PRICE OF SCRAP ALUMINUM.

THEY GIVE A YANK TO MAKE SURE THE LEAD WIRE'S BEEN SEVERED

AND THEN, IN A MOMENT, UNDO WHAT SOME NAMELESS TV REPAIRMAN TOOK HOURS TO ACCOMPLISH.

ONE ELDER BOY SWEARS THAT ON A MOONLIT NIGHT HE SAW THE GHOSTLY IMAGE OF A MAN WHO MODERATED A GAME SHOW

WHICH HAS BEEN OFF THE AIR FOR TWENTY YEARS.

FROM A ROTARY OVEN IN THE BACK OF ZECHARIAH'S HOT NUT SHACK

THE SMELL OF FRESHLY ROASTED PEANUTS RISES THROUGH AN AIR SHAFT

AND INTO A THIRD-FLOOR NAVEL-JEWELRY SHOWROOM.

SNIFF SNIFF

LET'S GO SOMEWHERE ELSE.

THROUGH THE OFFICES SITUATED ON THIS AIR SHAFT PASS A SUCCESSION OF BUSINESSES

A BRASSIERE REBUILDER

SNIFF

DRIVEN TO FAILURE BY AN OTHERWISE PLEASANT SMELL.

A MANURE FUTURES BROKER

SNIFF

ON THOSE BRISK FALL DAYS

A FALSE EYEBROW IMPORTER

SNIFF

WHEN HUMAN APPETITES ARE EASILY PIQUED

A EUGENICS COUNSELOR

SNIFF

TWO MEN WORK THE OVEN FROM DAWN TILL DUSK.

TAKE A NUMBER!

ZECHARIAH'S HOT NUT SHACK

LATE AT NIGHT, ON A QUIET CITY STREET,

A 1991 CHERUB WITH A CARELESSLY REFOLDED MAP ON THE FRONT SEAT...

A PARKED-CAR READER PLIES HIS TRADE.

BELONGS TO AN UNHAPPY YOUNG MAN WITH A BLEAK FUTURE IN THE ORNAMENTAL TOOTHBRUSH BUSINESS.

A '73 MASTABA UPHOLSTERED IN BLACK ASTRAKHAN WOOL WITH A DASHBOARD STATUETTE OF MORRIS HILLQUIT...

BELONGS TO A RETIRED SOCIAL WORKER WHO IS FATED TO DIE IN THE EMBRACE OF A TEENAGE GIRLFRIEND.

AN '87 PELLAGRIN WITH A ROTTEN TAILPIPE...

ALL OF HIS POTENTIAL CUSTOMERS LIE ASLEEP IN THEIR NEARBY APARTMENTS.

BELONGS TO A WEALTHY WOMAN WHO WILL SLOWLY DISFIGURE HERSELF THROUGH OBSESSIVE HAIRPLUCKING.

A SUSPICIOUS DOORMAN CALLS THE POLICE.

A '92 SESAME CONVERTIBLE WITH A STRAW SOUVENIR HAT TOSSED IN THE BACK SEAT...

AT THE SIGHT OF THIS ILLUMINATED CAR, THE GIFTED SEER PRETENDS TO SEE NOTHING.

IN THE SHADOW OF A LARGE PUBLIC DENTAL CLINIC

STANDS A STOREFRONT CONCERN OF AN UNSPECIFIED NATURE.

BEHIND ITS HALF-CURTAINED WINDOWS REPOSE PILLARS OF ROCK CANDY AND LARGE PAPERED BALES OF TURKISH TAFFY,

FIFTY-GALLON DRUMS OF SEMI-SOFT CARAMEL AND ONE-THOUSAND-FOOT SPOOLS OF HEAVY-GAUGE LICORICE CABLE.

OCCASIONALLY, A POOR MAN STOPS TO LOOK IN,

HIS FACE STILL NUMB, A WORN APPOINTMENT CARD IN HIS SHIRT POCKET.

FEELING THAT THE DAMAGE HAS ALREADY BEEN DONE, HE DECIDES TO INDULGE HIS SWEET-TOOTH BEFORE TAKING THE SUBWAY,

I'D LIKE TWENTY-FIVE CENTS' WORTH OF ROCK CANDY.

SORRY, WHOLESALE ONLY.

A SIREN IN THE MIDDLE OF THE NIGHT

AROUSES VAGUE UNEASINESS AND IDLE CURIOSITY.

A FIRE? AN AMBULANCE? MAYBE SOMEONE I KNOW... SOUNDS LIKE IT'S IN THE NEIGHBORHOOD.

FORTUNATELY, A GROUP OF DEDICATED VOLUNTEERS

UNEMPLOYED ANESTHESIOLOGISTS, OFF-SEASON LIFEGUARDS, AMATEUR POLICEMEN...

GATHER EACH NIGHT IN A RENT-FREE OFFICE, EQUIPPED WITH A SHORT-WAVE RADIO, TO MONITOR THE EVENING'S ASSORTED SIRENS AND ALARMS.

52-YEAR-OLD WHITE MALE, CORONARY THROMBOSIS AT 352 UVULA ST.

FORCED ENTRY AT THE MOLDAU GIFT SHOP.

THE MEMBERS OF THE SIREN QUERY BRIGADE ARE A HEARTY LOT WHO THRIVE ON LITTLE SLEEP AND THE MISFORTUNES OF OTHERS.

35-YEAR-OLD HISPANIC FEMALE, CANNED-SOUP POISONING AT 11 ALBINO AVENUE.

FIST FIGHT AT THE SPHINX HOTEL.

A CALL COMES IN

WHAT WAS THAT SIREN A MINUTE AGO? IT WOKE ME UP.

AND WITHIN MOMENTS RECEIVES A SURE AND COMFORTING REPLY.

IT'S A ONE-ALARM FIRE AT THE FRICASSEE CLUB ON PASTORAL AVENUE.

THE ANONYMOUS CALLER EXPRESSES HIS APPRECIATION

OH, I SEE. THANK YOU. GOOD NIGHT.

AND GOES BACK TO SLEEP.

THAT HAS NOTHING TO DO WITH ME.

MR. KNIPL HAD SEEN THESE SIGNS IN THE WINDOWS OF BLOCK-AND-TACKLE SHOPS AND ON THE GATES OF SCRAP-METAL YARDS

YEAR ROUND
SALVAGE BOAT
EXCURSIONS
EVERY SATURDAY 4 A.M
LEAVES FROM PIER 2
FOOT OF GREEGREE ST.
RAIN OR SHINE

BUT COULDN'T IMAGINE WHO WOULD GO.

AT THAT HOUR TO RETRIEVE SUNKEN PROPERTY?

AND YET, THERE ARE MEN, FROM ALL WALKS OF LIFE, WHO EAGERLY ANTICIPATE RISING BEFORE DAWN ON A SATURDAY MORNING,

A LIGHT SUPPER AT FIVE AND IN BED BY EIGHT.

DRESSING IN THEIR IDEA OF SALVAGE MAN'S GARB

STEEL REINFORCED BOOTS, OILSKIN JACKET AND GOGGLES.

AND PACKING A LUNCH TO SPEND THE DAY ON A TRAWLER ANCHORED IN THE CITY'S LOWER BAY.

THE EXCURSION LEADER HAS AN OBJECT IN MIND

A PORTABLE BAR WHICH ROLLED OFF THE AFTERDECK OF THE MARIA CAECUM, NEW YEAR'S EVE 1928.

AND AT THAT HOUR OF THE DAY IS ABLE TO IMBUE ANYTHING WITH THE IRRESISTIBLE AURA

A FULL BAR, STOCKED FOR THE EVENING.

WHATEVER COMES UP WE SPLIT EIGHT WAYS.

OF THE LOST JUST WAITING TO BE FOUND.

WHAT'D YOU BRING FOR LUNCH?

AT WHAT POINT IN THE WAR AGAINST DISEASE

WERE INDIVIDUALLY WRAPPED, SANITARY DRINKING STRAWS BROUGHT INTO PLAY ON THE FRONTLINE?

1960 ...1962?

MR. KNIPL ONCE THOUGHT HE COULD TRACE A CHILDHOOD CASE OF BRONCHITIS

1961?

TO AN OVERLY HANDLED BOX OF STRAWS KEPT NEXT TO THE CASH REGISTER AT A LOCAL CANDYSTORE —

HOCK HOCK

SEVEN-INCH-LONG PAPER TUBES OF VARIOUS PASTEL HUES

BLOOD & SAWDUST BRAND CIRKUS 5 STRAWS SANITIZED FOR YOUR HEALTH

100 COUNT ASST. COLORS

OF A DELICACY COMPARABLE TO THAT OF THE BRONCHIOLES OF A CHILD'S LUNG,

THESE POOR, MAN-MADE EXTENSIONS OF THE HUMAN BREATHING APPARATUS COULD BARELY HELP ONE THROUGH A BOTTLE OF SODA,

MUCH LESS AN EPIDEMIC OF INFLUENZA.

HOCK HOCK

A NEW UPSTAIRS NEIGHBOR GOES BAREFOOT ON LINOLEUM COVERED FLOORS.

MUST BE A WOMAN, AGE THIRTY-NINE, FIVE-FOOT SIX INCHES TALL, ONE HUNDRED AND FORTY POUNDS, SIZE SEVEN NARROW SHOE.

TAM TAM TAMP TE TAMP

BUT WHO WANTS TO KNOW EXACTLY WHERE SHE IS AT EVERY MOMENT? THAT SHE GOES TO THE REFRIGERATOR IN THE MIDDLE OF THE NIGHT?

I'LL MAKE HER A PRESENT OF A PAIR OF SLIPPERS.

"MONTE CARLO SOURDINES" SIZE SEVEN.

THEY'RE FOR SOMEONE I'VE NEVER MET.

ARE YOU AWARE THAT IN CERTAIN CULTURES SUCH A GIFT IS TABOO? SHE MAY HAVE A JEALOUS FIANCÉ OR BE A WIDOW IN MOURNING. WHAT DO YOU KNOW FOR SURE?

I CAN HEAR EVERY STEP SHE TAKES.

AND WHAT GUARANTEE DO YOU HAVE THAT SHE'LL ADOPT THE WEARING OF SLIPPERS FOR YOUR BENEFIT? SHE MAY GO BAREFOOT FOR REASONS OF HEALTH.

AND IF SHE ACCEPTS YOUR SELFISH GIFT, WHAT WILL YOU ASK OF HER NEXT? CORK-PANELED WALLS? LOW-PROFILE TOILETS? A TEN O'CLOCK CURFEW ON VEGETABLE PARING?

I'M WRONG...

SHE'S AT LEAST A SIZE EIGHT.

TAM TAM TAMP TE TAMP

AROUND THE TWENTY-FIFTH OF EACH MONTH, A SENSE OF IMPERMANENCE PERVADES THE CITY.

I WASN'T FINISHED WITH THAT COFFEE.

ESTIMATORS FROM WELL-KNOWN MOVING COMPANIES REDUCE HUMAN LIVES TO THEIR CUBIC SQUARE FOOTAGE.

WE CAN FIT YOU IN A TWENTY-EIGHT FOOTER.

THE NUMBER OF STEPS UP TO A LOBBY ENTRANCE BECOMES A DETERMINING FACTOR IN ONE'S FUTURE.

OTHERWISE HEALTHY INDIVIDUALS DEVELOP A MORBID FASCINATION WITH STRAPPING TAPE AND PADDED BLANKETS.

PEOPLE ARE FORCED TO CALCULATE, IN U.S. DOLLARS, THE SENTIMENTAL VALUE OF LARGE, UNWIELDY PIECES OF FURNITURE.

FAMILIAR BEDROOM VIEWS ARE FORSAKEN WITHOUT A THOUGHT.

THE EYES OF THE MIDDLE CLASS TURN, FOR COMFORT, TOWARD THE UNCHANGING PROFILE OF THE STREET CURB,

THAT FIVE-THOUSAND, SEVEN-HUNDRED-MILE-LONG MONUMENT COMMEMORATING THE SEPARATION OF SIDEWALK FROM GUTTER.

A SUDDEN DROP IN THE LEVEL OF LIQUID SOAP IN DISPENSERS THROUGHOUT THE APRICOT TOWER:

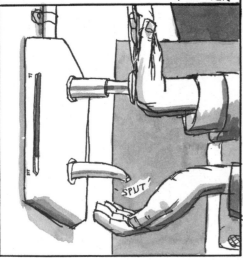

THE SUPERINTENDENT OF THE COMPOTE CENTER IS BESIEGED WITH COMPLAINTS.

IT CAN'T BE! THEY'RE ALL FED BY A ROOF-TOP RESERVOIR.

12TH FLOOR LADIES IN THE PEAR HOUSE NEEDS SOAP.

EXECUTIVES RELUCTANTLY LEAVE THEIR REST ROOMS HAVING ONLY WASHED WITH HOT WATER.

AT NOON, THE CAUSE IS ANNOUNCED.

A RUPTURE SOMEWHERE IN THE MAIN OF OUR CENTRALIZED SYSTEM.

EMERGENCY VALVES ARE CLOSED; JANITORS, ELEVATOR OPERATORS AND PORTERS ARE PRESSED INTO A SEARCH FOR THE LEAK.

AH! CAN YOU SMELL IT? THAT'S THE RESERVOIR.

AT FOUR O'CLOCK, NOTHING HAVING BEEN RESOLVED, BARS OF SOAP ARE DISTRIBUTED THROUGHOUT THE COMPLEX.

JUST BEFORE MIDNIGHT, THE OWNER OF A MEZZANINE SHAMPOO PARLOR IS CHARGED WITH HAVING ILLEGALLY TAPPED INTO THE MAIN FOR HIS OWN "PRIVATE USE."

IT'S A CITY-WIDE SCANDAL. HE SOLD THE STUFF WHOLESALE TO OTHER BUILDINGS. EVERYONE'S HANDS ARE DIRTY.

| A LONG-DISTANCE BUS LEAVES THE HIGHWAY | TO MAKE ANOTHER STOP ON THE MAIN STREET OF ANOTHER STUNTED CITY. | A FEW PASSENGERS SEARCH THE PASSING STOREFRONTS FOR A SIGN. | TWO FOOT-SOLDIERS IN "THE CONSOLATION ARMY," |

| THAT PHILANTHROPIC ORGANIZATION, SET UP ON MILITARY LINES, TO ENCOURAGE FLIRTATION, COITION AND COMMON-LAW MARRIAGE, | SUDDENLY LOSE THEIR NERVE, | | TO KILL THE TIME, A YOUNG CIVIL ENGINEER SHOWS MR. KNIPL HIS GRANDIOSE PLANS FOR BRIDGES WHICH WILL NEVER BE BUILT. |

TWO FOOT SOLDIERS IN THE CONSOLATION ARMY LAUNCH THEIR SIEGE OF NEW EDEMA FROM THE MEN'S ROOM OF THE LOCAL BUS STATION.

TO RID OURSELVES OF THE SMELL OF BUS.

THEY REPORT TO AN ANCIENT FIELD OFFICE

WHERE THEY'RE ASSIGNED AN UNDERCOVER DAY JOB

YOU PAY THE ELECTRIC BILL AND IT DOES EVERYTHING ELSE.

AND A FURNISHED ROOM EQUIPPED WITH HEAVY-GAUGE BED LINENS.

AFTER NIGHTFALL, THEY RECONNOITER THE PERIMETER OF BUFFET TABLES AT THE TOWN'S VARIOUS SOCIAL FUNCTIONS.

EVENTUALLY, ONE INNOCENT CIVILIAN IS BEATEN INTO SUBMISSION BY GOOD-NATURED, FRANK CONVERSATION.

THEY SAY IT'S MORE IMPORTANT TO CHOOSE THE RIGHT MATE THAN TO CHOOSE YOUR OWN PARENTS.

YES, SOME PEOPLE BELIEVE THAT THE ORGANS OF TASTE AND SMELL ARE ACTIVE BEFORE BIRTH.

THE PASSIONATE EMBRACES WHICH FOLLOW ARE MADE ACCORDING TO THE INSTRUCTIONS OF A HANDBOOK PUBLISHED IN 1957.

FOR THE NEXT FIVE YEARS, OR UNTIL A COMMON-LAW MARRIAGE IS WITHIN SIGHT, A SOLDIER CANNOT STOP FOR A MOMENT TO QUESTION WHETHER HIS EFFORTS ARE, IN FACT, OFFERING THE SLIGHTEST CONSOLATION TO ANYONE.

Panel 1: TOWARD THE CLOSE OF EACH BUSINESS DAY, A MAN COMES AROUND

Panel 2: OFFERING TO REMOVE AND EXPUNGE UNWANTED TEXTUAL MATTER.

Panel 3: FROM AN EMBARRASSING MEMOIR TO AN IMPRUDENT SIGNATURE

Panel 4: HE CARRIES A BLUE BOTTLE OF HIGHLY POTENT CHLORINE BLEACH AND A DELICATE GLASS WAND.

Panel 5: FROM A FEW LOVE LETTERS TO A DECADE'S WORTH OF CORPORATE LEDGERS

Panel 6: A TRUCK AND DRIVER FOLLOW BEHIND AT A DISCREET DISTANCE.

Panel 7: IN A SHED ON THE OUTSKIRTS OF THE CITY

Panel 8: AN ASSORTMENT OF DOCUMENTS ARE LEFT TO SOAK OVERNIGHT OR UNTIL DEVOID OF MEANING.

HE WAS NOT THE ONLY YOUNG MAN TO FALL PREY TO THE LURE OF ESCALATOR RIDING —

SKEWS ME, SKEWS ME

TO SPEND THE BUSINESS HOURS OF EACH DAY SEARCHING IN DEPARTMENT STORES AND HOTEL LOBBIES

I'VE SEEN THEM BEFORE.

COMIN' THROUGH!

FOR THE SOLE PURPOSE OF TAKING A RIDE,

FIRST FLOOR TO MEZZANINE IN BYNG BROS. DEPARTMENT STORE.

TO SAVOR THE LIFT AND DESCENT PECULIAR TO EACH MACHINE,

THE WOODEN "TREPSMILL" IN THE REAR OF THE LAOCOÖN HOTEL.

TO WALK AHEAD AND FEEL THE COMBINED FORCE OF ONE'S FOOT MEETING A RISING TREAD

THE HIGH-SPEED "OPHIR" IN THE LOBBY OF 527 MYSIA AVENUE.

OR TO INDUCE A MOMENT OF GIDDY STASIS BY WALKING UP A DOWN ESCALATOR.

THE SELF-STARTING "SHPOTZIR" FROM THE SUBWAY RIGHT INTO THE FIXSHON TOWER.

STEP ON ESCALATOR TO START

WHILE A FEW IMAGINED THAT THEY MIGHT SOMEDAY WIN THE SPONSORSHIP OF A FAMOUS MANUFACTURER AND CONTINUE RIDING ON A PROFESSIONAL BASIS,

MOST DID NOT LOOK BEYOND THE VANISHING POINT OF TREAD AND RISER,

TOWARD THE END OF A PERFECT DANISH, MR. KNIPL DISCOVERS... A PLUM STEM? AN ALMOND HUSK?

NO, A CLOSED STAPLE.

IN MY PRUNE DANISH.

I CAN EXPLAIN.

EACH NIGHT, MY BAKER SHOWS UP WITH A NEW DIAGNOSIS FROM THE DEPARTMENT OF HEALTH STAPLED TO HIS WORK PERMIT. YOU HAVE NO IDEA OF THE PAPER WORK INVOLVED WHEN YOU HAVE A SICK EMPLOYEE.

AND THEN THE INSPECTORS FROM THE PASTRY COMMISSION MAKE THEIR SURPRISE VISITS TO LOOK FOR VIOLATIONS AND POST LONG-FORGOTTEN "STANDARDS OF TASTE" IN HEAT-RESISTANT FRAMES NEXT TO THE OVEN.

"ON AND AFTER JANUARY FIRST, NINETEEN HUNDRED AND THIRTY-FIVE, ALL PRUNE DANISH SHALL BE GLAZED WITH A STANDARD EGG WASH... IN ALL CASES, THESE PASTRIES SHALL NOT EXCEED FIVE AND ONE-HALF INCHES IN WIDTH AND BE FILLED TO A DEPTH OF NO LESS THAN ONE-QUARTER INCH WITH CERTIFIED PRUNE PURÉE (SEE SECTION 7.4)..."

OF COURSE, THEY CAN BE BRIBED. YOU'VE SEEN THOSE OVERLY-GLAZED, PEEKABOO-STYLE MONSTROSITIES IN COFFEE SHOP WINDOWS.

AND NOW, MY EXTERMINATOR TELLS ME THAT FOR EACH COCKROACH HE KILLS, I NEED A NOTARIZED DEATH CERTIFICATE.

BUT NOT EVERYONE IS AS CAREFUL AS YOU ARE... A LAWSUIT FROM A CUSTOMER WHO SWALLOWED A PAPER CLIP.

A PHYSIOGNOMIST WANDERS THE CITY IN SEARCH OF AN AUTHENTIC FACIAL EXPRESSION.

THEY'RE ALL BAD ACTORS HERE.

I ORDERED THIS ON RYE.

HE FLEES FROM POOR IMITATIONS OF 1950s TELEVISION ACTING —

TONIGHT WE HAVE FOR YOU A VERY DISTURBING STORY...

THAT MAN WAS RAISED ON "THE OLEOMARGARINE HOUR." STARRING NUCHAL FEYROL.

THOSE FACIAL EXPRESSIONS BASED, IN TURN, UPON A FEW NINETEENTH-CENTURY THEATRICAL CONVENTIONS, WHICH SOMEHOW SURVIVED INTO THE EARLY YEARS OF MOTION PICTURES.

THAT SAME SAD GRIMACE OF INCOMPREHENSION SEEN IN PRINTS OF THE COMMEDIA DELL'ARTE.

UNMINDFUL OF THE DANGERS INVOLVED, HE SEEKS OUT, INSTEAD, THOSE EXTRAORDINARY SITUATIONS

THE CASHIER AT THE BUREAU OF VITAL STATISTICS

HE'S NOT THE ONLY MAURICE KULCRIM WHO DIED ON APRIL 15, 1971.

IN WHICH THE HUMAN FACE IS FORCED OUT OF THE WELL-WORN RUT OF CAUSE AND EFFECT,

THE FIVE-AND-TEN-CENT-STORE DEMONSTRATOR OF EYEGLASS DEFOGGER.

NOW I CAN'T SEE A THING.

24 OZ. TUBE $1.75

IT WORKS REALLY

WHERE FACIAL MUSCLES ARE TWISTED INTO NEVER-BEFORE-SEEN CONFIGURATIONS,

THE SIDEWALK DICTIONARY AND THESAURUS SALESMAN.

DOES IT HAVE "DROSOPHILA"?

50,000 WORDS

WHERE FERAL DOGS ARE STOPPED IN THEIR TRACKS

A FOREIGN SAILOR ON SHORE LEAVE TRYING TO DECIPHER A LOCAL PARKING SIGN.

"PTOLEMY ZONE... NO MOVING"

ON THE OUTSKIRTS OF HUMAN EMOTION.

A MAN WATCHING TELEVISON ON THE EIGHTH FLOOR OF A DEPARTMENT STORE.

...CONCERNING OUR BRIEF LIFE CYCLE AND GREAT REPRODUCTIVE POWERS!

WHOEVER THOUGHT THAT THESE UTOPIAN IMPULSES WOULD BE FIRST EXPRESSED BY THE MOST DESPERATE OF SMALL BUSINESSMEN

I THOUGHT IT WAS A TRICK, TO LURE THEM IN HALF-ASLEEP AND HUNGRY...

AND AT SUCH AN EARLY HOUR OF THE DAY?

BUT, YOU SEE, IT'S FOR REAL!

THAT CUSTOMERS WOULD FLOCK IN CELEBRATION OF THE GRADUAL WITHERING OF THE PROFIT MOTIVE

TWO EGGS, HOME FRIES, TOAST, COFFEE AND ORANGE JUICE... A DOLLAR TWENTY-NINE!

WHAT CAN THEY MAKE, FIFTY CENTS, A QUARTER?

AND THE HAPPY STANDARDIZATION OF THE BREAKFAST MENU FOR THE BENEFIT OF THE GREATEST NUMBER OF PEOPLE?

IF YOU WANT BACON, YOU'LL HAVE TO PAY EXTRA FOR IT.

THE LONG, DARK COUNTERS AT WHICH THEY ONCE ATE DIRTY EGGS AND DRANK IMITATION ORANGE JUICE

FOR A YEAR AND A HALF, I WENT TO LYPOMA'S... WHO KNEW ANY BETTER?

HAVE BEEN RELEGATED TO A BENIGHTED PERIOD OF BRUTISH STRUGGLE.

IT WAS ON MY WAY FROM THE SUBWAY AND WHO HAD THE STRENGTH TO LOOK FURTHER?

FORGET ABOUT IT, FORGET IT.

EVERY FEW MONTHS, ANOTHER INSPIRED RESTAURATEUR WILL COME FORTH WITH A PROPOSAL FOR A NEW, MORE PERFECT, BREAKFAST SPECIAL

FOR THE SAME DOLLAR TWENTY-NINE, I GIVE YOU TWO EGGS, A FULL ORDER OF TOAST (TWO SLICES, YOUR CHOICE WHITE OR WHOLE WHEAT), HOME FRIES, COFFEE AND ORANGE JUICE!

THE WONDERFUL DETAILS OF WHICH NO CUSTOMER CAN YET CONCEIVE.

ONE PIECE OF TOAST?

WHAT DO YOU WANT FOR A DOLLAR TWENTY-NINE?

DURING THE SECOND ACT OF A LIGHT OPERETTA, HIS KEY CHAIN BEGINS TO CHAFE AGAINST HIS THIGH.

I SHOULD HAVE KNOWN.

LIKE THOUSANDS OF OTHER UNFORTUNATE SOULS WHO SPEND A LIFETIME IN FAILED ATTEMPTS AT ESCAPE,

EXCUSE ME, EXCUSE ME.

CARMINE DELAPS REMAINS FETTERED TO HIS ONE-BEDROOM APARTMENT BY SEVERAL SHORT LENGTHS OF BEAD CHAIN —

BEAD CHAIN, BALL CHAIN, CALL IT WHAT YOU LIKE...

THAT TWENTIETH-CENTURY SHACKLE, CONSISTING OF TINY METAL BEADS LINKED THROUGH THEIR CORE BY MINUTE STEEL RODS.

AFTER FOURTEEN YEARS IN CAPTIVITY, ONE CAN'T JUST "GO OUT" FOR THE EVENING.

EACH CHAIN CAN BE CLOSED UPON ITSELF, OR LENGTHENED TO INFINITY, BY MEANS OF A SIMPLE CLASP.

AND TO THINK THEY ALLOW CHILDREN TO PLAY WITH THESE THINGS!

IN THIS CASE, ONE SHORT LENGTH EXTENDS FROM HIS PANT'S POCKET TO HIS FRONT DOOR.

JUST LONG ENOUGH TO CREATE THE ILLUSION OF FREEDOM.

ANOTHER TETHERS THE FINGERTIPS OF HIS RIGHT HAND TO THE ELECTRICAL SWITCH ON HIS NIGHT-TABLE LAMP.

LAST SUNDAY'S PAPER, STILL UNREAD.

A THIRD CHAIN HANGS UNSEEN, LINKING THE LEVER OF HIS TOILET TO A PLUG IN THE DEPTHS OF ITS PORCELAIN RESERVOIR.

♫ "GYVES THAT NO SMITH CAN WELD, NO RUST DEVOUR!" ♫

AT A QUARTER PAST ELEVEN, THE EATING AND CONVERSATION COME TO AN END.

THE REMAINING DINERS LOWER THEIR GAZE IN CONTEMPLATION OF LAST THINGS.

A PIECE OF BRISKET LOST IN THE SHADOW OF A DESSERT PLATE.

UNUTTERABLE VERITIES, HOPELESS ESTIMATIONS AND SAD FACTS

A GROUP OF UNDESIRABLE FRENCH FRIES STAINED WITH KETCHUP.

ARE MADE MANIFEST IN THE DETAILS OF A DIRTY TABLE.

A WEDGE OF SOUR TOMATO REFLECTED IN A POOL OF COLE SLAW DRESSING.

THE TEN-THOUSANDTH VARI-ATION UPON AN ARRANGEMENT KNOWN SINCE CHILDHOOD.

A GLASS OF TEA WOBBLING ON THE LINK-KNOT OF A "SPECIAL" FRANKFURTER.

THE CHECK IS PAID, A TIP CALCULATED AND THE BUSBOY SLIPPED A TEN-DOLLAR BILL

PLEASE, WAIT AT LEAST UNTIL WE'VE GONE A FEW BLOCKS, OUT OF EARSHOT, BEFORE YOU CLEAR THE TABLE.

AS THOUGH THESE REVELATIONS OF THE EVENING COULD BE WIPED AWAY IN A MOMENT

READY? LET'S GO.

BY A YOUNG MAN WORKING FOR THE MINIMUM WAGE.

THROUGH THE NINE FULLY AIR-CON-
DITIONED ACRES OF FLOOR SPACE
IN THIS ONCE-PREMIER EXHIBITION
CENTER,

BUSY
OVER THERE
TONIGHT.

WE'RE TAKING
DOWN THE "FANCY
FUMIGATING AND
MOSQUITO BREEDERS
GIFT SHOW"..

THERE PASSES AN INCONCEIVABLE
ARRAY OF EVER-MORE-DISMAL
TRADE SHOWS AND EXPOSITIONS,

AND SETTING
UP THE "4th
INTERNATIONAL
EVAPORATED
MILK FAIR"

BY MEANS OF HIGH-SPEED
FREIGHT ELEVATORS,

ON MONDAY,
THE "MONOGRAMMED
PAJAMA AND
SMELLING SALTS
FRANCHISE SHOW"
COMES IN...

OFF-STREET LOADING DOCKS AND
OIL-GREASED TRUCK RAMPS,

WITH A MODEL
COIN-OPERATED
LAUNDROMAT
COMPLETE WITH
SOILED CLOTHING
FROM AROUND THE
WORLD.

THE VARIOUS HALLS CAN BE
TRANSFORMED, OVERNIGHT,
INTO GLITTERING CONSUMER
WONDERLANDS—

TUESDAY
NIGHT, THE
"LARGE-SIZE-
SHOE RETAILERS
OF NORTH AMERICA"
COME IN...

THIS YEAR
EVERYTHING'S
CARDBOARD!

ALL FOR THE BRIEF DURATION
OF A TWO-DAY EXPOSITION!

WITH A
WALK-THRU
TROPICAL
"CHEAP-LABOR
VILLAGE."

IT IS ONLY UPON LEAVING THAT
THE VISITOR BEGINS TO FEEL
THE BURDEN OF PROMOTIONAL
LITERATURE

LATER
IN THE WEEK
WE HAVE THE
"HOLIDAY NOISE-
MAKER SHOW;"
A "EUROPEAN
NEUROPATH'S
EXPOSITION"...

AND NOTICES THAT HIS OWN HEART
HAS NEARLY BEEN TRANSFIXED BY THE
PIN OF A COMPLIMENTARY NAME TAG.

THE
"LINOLEUM
LAYER'S HOBBY
EXTRAVAGANZA"
AND A "NEGLIGEE
RECYCLING SHOW."

MR. KNIPL IS SURPRISED TO SEE THIS MOVIE STILL PLAYING IN A SMALL SIDE-STREET THEATER.

IT'S BEEN HERE SINCE CHRISTMAS OF LAST YEAR...

FLORA

THE ASCENDING COLON

WITH HORACE BISMUTH AND VIVIAN SCYBALA

FOUR SHOWINGS DAILY, SOMETIMES TO A FULL HOUSE.

I DIDN'T SEE IT, BUT I REMEMBER, LAST WINTER, IT CAME OUT, PLAYED AROUND TOWN FOR A FEW WEEKS AND THEN DISAPPEARED.

HELD OVER INDEFINITELY. NEXT SHOW AT SEVEN-THIRTY.

IT'S THE STORY OF A YOUNG SURGEON-COLONEL OF THE BRITISH OCCUPATION FORCES IN ADEN AND HIS HEROIC, BUT FUTILE, SEARCH FOR A CASE OF CONSTIPATION AMONG THE NATIVE POPULATION.

PLEASE FORM A LINE TO THE RIGHT SO AS NOT TO OBSTRUCT THE SIDEWALK!

THINK OF ALL THE FILMS THAT CAME AND WENT SINCE THEN, A WHOLE WORLD OF COMEDY, ADVENTURE, TRAGEDY.

THE LIDS OF THE DISUSED ASH-TRAYS BEHIND EACH SEAT VIBRATE IN SYMPATHY AT CERTAIN POINTS IN THE FILM'S SOUNDTRACK.

THESE MEN YOU SEE HERE WILL NEVER VOLUNTARILY LIVE WHERE PEOPLE ARE NOT PERMITTED TO EVACUATE THEIR BOWELS IN PUBLIC! NEVER!

THE THEATER'S MANAGER EXPLAINS...

THERE WILL ALWAYS BE AN AUDIENCE FOR A FILM LIKE "THE ASCENDING COLON." EACH YEAR A NEW GROUP OF MOVIEGOERS WILL COME OF AGE AND SEEK OUT JUST SUCH AN ENTERTAINMENT. NO ADVERTISING IS REQUIRED.

WHEN THE VIEWER IS READY, HE OR SHE WILL KNOW WHERE TO GO.

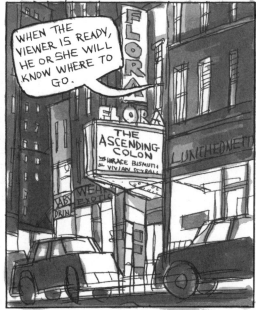

REGARDLESS OF THE OCCASION, TIME OF DAY OR METHOD OF APPROACH,

HOW COULD I REFUSE THE INVITATION? HE'S OWED ME MONEY FOR SIX MONTHS.

EACH VISITOR TO THIS APARTMENT BUILDING MUST STEEL HIMSELF AGAINST THE SHORT, PITIFUL CRY OF THE FRONT DOOR BUZZER.

APARTMENT 6-F. ARNOLD VEENIAL, ARNOLD VEENIAL...

HAS THE SOUND OF THIS PRIMITIVE BRASS LARYNX RISEN IN PITCH OR ALTERED IN TIMBRE AFTER SEVEN DECADES OF CONSTANT USE?

U.S. PAT. N°

ASK THE FIRST SUPERINTENDENT'S SON, NOW LIVING IN RETIREMENT,

EAAAAAAY

OR A DELIVERY BOY OF THAT TIME, LATELY SUFFERING FROM DEMENTIA, IF THEY CAN REMEMBER.

AND FOR WHAT REASON WAS THIS MOST TENDER ORIFICE IN THE BUILDING'S STRUCTURE GIVEN A VOICE?

I FELT THAT I SHOULD APOLOGIZE IN PERSON...

(NOW, A WOEFUL BLEAT ASSOCIATED WITH FOREDOOMED ENTERPRISES.)

FOR NOT YET BEING ABLE TO PAY OFF MY OUTSTANDING DEBT.

TO ANSWER THE THIN, NASAL SCREAM FROM THE FOYER OF AN APARTMENT SIX FLOORS ABOVE.

AH! THAT MUST BE HIM!

ENNNNNGK

UPSTAIRS, IN THE OFFICE OF A TEMPORARY LABOR CONTRACTOR...

YOU NEED TWENTY-FIVE MEN, WITH CLEAN HANDS, TO BREAK IN THE ZIPPERS ON A TRUCKLOAD OF MEN'S SLACKS? 6 A.M. SUNDAY MORNING, RAIN OR SHINE? NO PROBLEM.

IT IS A THRILLING SIGHT. TWENTY-FIVE MEN APPEAR OUT OF NOWHERE, PERFORM A SET PHYSICAL TASK, AND THEN, JUST AS SUDDENLY, DISAPPEAR.

SEVENTY MEN, WITH THEIR OWN RUBBER BOOTS, TO EXCAVATE AN ABANDONED TUNA SALAD BASIN IN MID-TOWN.

TWELVE MEN TO SWAB THE MARQUEE AND TURN OVER THE SIDEWALK IN FRONT OF A PSYCHIATRIC HOSPITAL.

DOES THE AUDIENCE AT A BALLET WORRY ABOUT THE DANCERS' HEALTH INSURANCE AND PENSION PLAN?

ADMISSION'S FREE! NO TICKET REQUIRED!

DOWNSTAIRS, IN A TICKET BROKER'S STALL...

PEOPLE SPEND THEIR LUNCH HOUR WATCHING MEN UNLOAD A TRUCK OF SLACKS, ON THEIR WAY HOME, THEY'LL STOP AGAIN TO WATCH A GANG OF MEN DIVERT A FLOOD OF COFFEE IN THE STREET.

COMMON LABORERS PAID A MINIMUM WAGE BY THE DAY, NO BENEFITS, NO RECORDS —CASH! ADD TO THAT THE COST OF PORTABLE BLEACHERS AND ADVERTISING AND YOUR BEST SEAT WOULD GO FOR, TOPS, THIRTY-FIVE DOLLARS.

THERE'S A VAST UNTAPPED AUDIENCE FOR THIS SORT OF SPECTACLE...

BUT THE IMPRESARIO OF HUMAN DRUDGERY HAS NOT YET BEEN BORN.

THE SOLE SURVIVING SON OF AL MOONER DRIVES AIMLESSLY THROUGH MID-TOWN IN HIS FATHER'S OLD CAR.

TWO HOURS UPSTATE WAS DEEP IN THE COUNTRY...

A FADED, OBLONG CARD HANGS BY FRAGILE WIRES FROM THE REAR BUMPER.

TOURISTS WERE STARVED FOR DIVERSION... ANYTHING.

I Escaped from... AL MOONER'S PYGMY Penitentiary ROUTE 17 • DEWLAP, USA

MY FATHER BUILT IT WITH HIS OWN HANDS ON A THREE-ACRE LOT — A WORMY ORCHARD. LATH AND STAFF PLASTER TOPPED WITH REAL BARBED WIRE. AT NIGHT IT WAS A FAIRY-LAND OF SEARCHLIGHTS AND ELECTRIC SIRENS.

ON THE QUARTER HOUR HE STAGED FULL-SCALE RIOTS, ATTEMPTED BREAK-OUTS, YARD EXERCISES, AND ELECTROCUTIONS. THE GIFT SHOP SOLD STRIPED PAJAMAS AND GAG LICENSE PLATES.

AS A TEENAGER, I WORKED THE PARKING LOT WITH A PAIR OF PLIERS.

IN SEASON, WE EMPLOYED THREE DOZEN REAL EX-CONVICTS, ALL UNDER FIVE FEET TALL; THE GUARDS WERE COLLEGE KIDS ON VACATION.

THEN, IN THE SUMMER OF 1968, THEY MADE MY FATHER A GOOD OFFER FOR THE LAND. MY BROTHER AND I HAD TERRIBLE ALLERGIES, AND SO, AFTER FIFTEEN YEARS OF HARD LABOR, HE LET EVERYONE GO. THERE WERE NO HARD FEELINGS.

LOOK, BY THEN EVERYBODY HAD SEEN IT — THE NOVELTY WAS GONE. ON A HOT WEEKDAY AFTERNOON THERE WERE SOME-TIMES MORE PEOPLE BEHIND BARS THAN WALKING FREE.

MR. KNIPL SEEKS RELIEF FROM AN EARACHE.

FIVE YEARS AGO IT WORKED PERFECTLY, BUT NOW, SUDDENLY, NOTHING.

THERE'S ONLY ONE LISTING IN THE PHONE BOOK...

"SHESHELL ELECTRIC HEATING PADS, FACTORY AUTHORIZED REPAIR AND SERVICE..." 211 DITTANY AVE."

SURE, I HAVE ALL THE PAPERS: DIPLOMAS FROM THE MOLLUSK MANUFACTURING COMPANY, SUMMER 1967 COURSE IN TROUBLESHOOTING AND CUSTOMER RELATIONS, SIX-WEEK INTENSIVE TRAINING AT THE MOLLUSK INSTITUTE IN 1972, SEMINARS EVERY YEAR TO KEEP UP WITH THE NEW MODELS.

BUT MOST HEATING PADS GO FROM OLD AGE. THEY DRY OUT, THE ELEMENTS CAN'T BEAR THE CURRENT. REPAIR IS OUT OF THE QUESTION, THERE'S NOTHING WE CAN DO. SOMEONE HAS TO BREAK THE NEWS TO THE OWNER, COMMISERATE, OFFER DISCARD COUNSELING.

SOME PADS HAVE BEEN IN THE FAMILY FOR TWENTY-FIVE YEARS, AND THEN SUDDENLY IT'S TIME TO THROW IT OUT AND BUY A NEW ONE. SURE YOU'LL MISS THE OLD-STYLE, NIGHT-LIGHT CONTROL, THE SOUR SMELL OF RADIANT ELECTRIC HEAT, THE FAMILIAR BUZZ AND CLICK OF CURRENT — THESE ARE CHILDHOOD ASSOCIATIONS!

AT FIRST THEY QUESTION MY AUTHORITY — "WHO ARE YOU TO SAY IT'S FINISHED, WITHOUT EVEN TAKING A LOOK?.. FIVE YEARS AGO, WHEN I LAST USED IT, IT WORKED FINE." AH! A CUSTOMER.

GOOD AFTERNOON. COME IN, SIT DOWN. WHAT CAN I DO FOR YOU? LET'S TALK.

GONE ARE THE SMALL, HIGH-CLASS, NEIGHBORHOOD GROCERY STORES OFF ROMAN BOULEVARD.

ARE YOU HUNGRY?

PRIAPUS VIDEO

THE VALUED CUSTOMERS WHO CAME, BY INVITATION, TO EVENING TASTINGS OF NEW AND INTERESTING CANNED FOODS ARE NO MORE.

I'LL OPEN A CAN OF JELLIED GREEN-TURTLE CONSOMMÉ OR SEEDLESS GRAPES IN HEAVY SYRUP... WHATEVER YOU WANT.

ON THOSE WEEKDAY NIGHTS IN THE FALL, AFTER REGULAR BUSINESS HOURS, A BACK ROOM WOULD BE SET UP WITH CHAFING DISHES, TOOTHPICKS AND CAN OPENERS.

GOOD EVENING.

Fancy FOODS QUALITY IMPORTS

EXTRA FANCY

THESE WERE RECENT SHIPMENTS FROM OTHER LATITUDES OR SPECIALTY ITEMS AVAILABLE FOR THE FIRST TIME IN LIMITED QUANTITIES.

KAZBAH BRAND FRENCH ROOSTER COMBS IN 1¾ OZ. TINS; NEXT O'KIN BRAND BONELESS, SKINLESS AND FLESHLESS SARDINES IN PURE OLIVE OIL...

CUSTOMERS WERE ENCOURAGED TO BUY A CASE OR TWO AT A DISCOUNT PRICE; TO STOCK UP NOW FOR FUTURE HOME ENTERTAINMENTS.

QUISLING BROS. PRE-WAR-STYLE SAUERKRAUT IN 17 OZ. CANS; EXILE BRAND SLICED OX TONGUE IN 15 OZ. TINS...

FEINSHMECKER COCKTAIL FRANKS

ALBINO ASPARAGUS

FASCES QUALITY

ENLARGED ARTICHOKE HEARTS

EXILE BRAND
OX-TONGUE SLICED 48-15 OZ. CANS

THERE WERE, IT WAS SAID, BETTER YEARS FOR CERTAIN ITEMS.

PIA MATER BRAND, WHOLE BONED TURKEY IN AN 8 LB., 6 OZ. CAN FROM 1967.

ANY STOCK LEFT FROM '66?

PIA MAT

A TRUE CONNOISSEUR WOULD APPRECIATE THE DISCONTINUED BRAND, THE QUAINT, OUT-OF-STYLE LABEL

MY FATHER BOUGHT ALL THIS BACK IN 1968 — I THINK IT'S STILL GOOD.

ORPHANAGE BRAND

NET WT. 15½ OZ.

TENDER SEEDLESS GRAPES

AND THE EMBOSSED LOT NUMBER ON EACH CAN.

WHATEVER YOU LIKE.

"EV 278W M321"?

LATE AT NIGHT, MR. KNIPL GOES TO CHECK HIS POST OFFICE BOX.

FROM THE COIN SLOTS OF THE LOBBY VENDING MACHINES THERE EMANATES THE SMELL OF RANCID FINGER GREASE.

WHO NEEDS ONE- AND TWO-CENT STAMPS?

IN THE MAIN HALL, TWO NIGHT WORKERS LIE UNCONSCIOUS— OVERCOME BY THE ACCUMULATED FUMES OF A DAY'S LICKED STAMPS AND ENVELOPE FLAPS.

FROM A CAGED WINDOW BLOWS COLD AIR BEARING THE TANG OF FRESHLY PRINTED JUNK MAIL.

THE AROMA OF FORTY THOUSAND POSTCARDS SATURATED BY THE SUN AND AIR OF DISTANT CLIMES

MINGLES WITH THE CHEAP PERFUME OF A HUNDRED THOUSAND COMMERCIAL LOVE LETTERS — ALL SORTED BY ZIP CODE.

THE FAINT ODOR OF A MONTH'S WORTH OF WANTED POSTERS UNDER GLASS

TAINTS THE OTHERWISE THRILLING SCENT OF YET-TO-BE-DELIVERED MAIL.

NOTHING.

THROUGH ITS FLEET OF FOUR HUNDRED TRUCKS, MANNED BY BONDED LIGHT-BULB CHANGERS AND SPECIALISTS IN CHEWING GUM REMOVAL,

THE NAME "VANTZ" BECAME, IN MR. KNIPL'S MIND, SYNONYMOUS WITH THE ROUTINE MAINTENANCE OF A CERTAIN MINIMUM OF ORDER AND CLEANLINESS IN THE CITY.

AND THEN, ONE RAINY OCTOBER NIGHT, HE NOTICES AN UNACCUSTOMED GLOOM, IN THE LOBBY OF THE VYAMEYER BUILDING.

A SHORT PARAGRAPH ON THE BUSINESS PAGE EXPLAINS WHAT HAPPENED.

"GUM SCRAPERS' UNION BOSS ELOPES WITH VANTZ EXEC."

BUT IT WAS AN INSTITUTION.

IT WAS A FLY-BY-NIGHT OPERATION.

NO DIFFERENT FROM A STOREFRONT RADIOLOGIST OR A MAIL-ORDER DIVINITY SCHOOL... ONLY IT TOOK THEM TWENTY-FIVE YEARS TO SET UP A CONVINCING FACADE.

THAT'S ALL OF MY ADULT LIFE.

THEY LEFT DOZENS OF MID-TOWN OFFICE BUILDINGS WITH DIRTY FLOORS, HUNDREDS OF UNIFORMED WORKERS WITHOUT A DECENT CHANGE OF CLOTHING.

THEY WERE JUST WAITING FOR THE RIGHT MOMENT— BELIEVE ME.

ON THOSE STREETS ZONED FOR CARNAL AMUSEMENT,

HERE, SEE FOR YOURSELF.

WEDGED BETWEEN THE CHILI CON CARNE STANDS AND THE HAND-PAINTED NECKTIE SHOPS,

NEEDS A MANICURE, BUT OTHERWISE UNTOUCHED.

ARE NARROW, CURTAINED STORE-FRONTS CATERING TO THE QUIET ENJOYMENT OF A HARMLESS ORAL HABIT.

AND THIS WEEK MARDUK SULTANA'S UP 3.37 POINTS.

HERE, IN THESE DELICATESSENS OF SUN-CURED HORN, SHELTERED FROM THE CENSORIOUS EYES OF THE GENERAL PUBLIC,

I TELL YOU, THERE IS NO MORE ACCURATE BAROMETER OF THE NATION'S ECONOMY THAN THE FINGERNAILS OF A LOW-LEVEL OFFICE WORKER.

GOOD EVENING, MR. TOCSIN.

ONE CAN REPOSE IN PRIVATE WITH A SALT SHAKER AND A PILE OF CURRENT NEWSMAGAZINES OR OTHER ANXIETY-PRODUCING LITERATURE.

I COME HERE EVERY DAY AFTER WORK. IF I SEE SO MUCH AS A NIBBLED CUTICLE I GET OUT.

UNLIKE THE OPIUM DENS OF THE NINETEENTH CENTURY, A VISIT LASTS NO MORE THAN FIFTEEN MINUTES

OF COURSE THERE ARE PSYCHOLOGICAL FACTORS, ABNORMAL COMPULSIONS, ETC., BUT ULTIMATELY IT'S ALL ECONOMICS.

OR THE TIME IT TAKES TO REACH THE QUICK OF SEVERAL NAILS.

EXCUSE ME.

HERE, IN THESE SNACK-BARS OF AUTO-CANNIBALISM, NOTHING GOES TO WASTE.

SELL, SELL, SELL!

MR. KNIPL'S NEIGHBOR HAS A HARD TIME CONVINCING HIMSELF THAT HE'S LOCKED THE DOOR OF HIS OFFICE.

I SHOULD GIVE IT ONE MORE TRY.

WHAT DOES HE HAVE IN THERE THAT'S SO VALUABLE?

YEP, IT'S LOCKED.

THIS ACT OF COMPULSION, PERFORMED EACH TIME HE GOES OUT—

FADED STEEL OFFICE EQUIPMENT.

BUT JUST TO MAKE SURE...

FIVE OR SIX TIMES A DAY,

A DUSTY ADDRESSING MACHINE.

YES, I LOCKED IT.

FOR SEVENTEEN YEARS—

A FILE CABINET CONTAINING THE NAMES AND ADDRESSES OF SOME TWENTY-FOUR THOUSAND PEOPLE WHO WERE MOMENTARILY BLINDED BY EATING GRAPEFRUIT WITH A SPOON.

SO LET'S MAKE SURE...

RESULTS IN THE DESTRUCTION OF THE DOORKNOB AND LOCK MECHANISM.

JUST LIKE THAT, SUDDENLY, IT FELL APART IN MY HANDS!

401 CITRIC ACID COUNCIL —

56   The Door-Knob Trier

Panel 1: AGAIN TODAY, MR. KNIPL IMAGINES THAT HE CAN HEAR THE PLAINTIVE CRY OF A TWELVE-NOON SIREN

Panel 2: FROM ITS RUSTED PERCH ON THE ROOF OF A SHOEHORN MANUFAC- TURING PLANT

Panel 3: ON THE OUTSKIRTS OF THE CITY.

Panel 4: ON THOSE STREETS WITHIN EARSHOT, MEN STOP TO REGULATE THEIR CHEAP WRISTWATCHES

Panel 5: AND TO VERIFY THEIR RECOLLECTIONS OF SANDWICHES MADE IN A PRE- DAWN KITCHEN LIGHT.

Panel 6: A SHEET-METAL WORKER IS ROUSED FROM HIS DREAM OF ANOTHER LIFE

AT A DESK IN AN OFFICE ON THE EIGHTH FLOOR...

DANGER

Panel 7: SO QUIET I CAN HEAR THE WORKINGS OF MY OWN GASTROINTESTINAL TRACT.

Panel 8: BY THE SAME MERCILESS BLARE.

NO WONDER I'M HUNGRY.

To monitor the wholesale migration of shirts, aprons and pants from one labor pool to another,

"Why should they wash what isn't theirs?"

The city's uniform and linen rental companies have adopted, by mutual agreement, a foolproof system of identification.

"The collar, hem or pocket of every garment is stamped with an indelible mark unique to each company."

How does a short-sleeved, snap-buttoned, white shirt leased to a midtown coffee shop turn up six months later on the back of a grilled-cheese presser, five hundred blocks away?

The custom-embroidered names and logos can be easily removed with a fresh razor blade.

In the midst of friendly small talk with a counterman or dishwasher,

"Before here, I worked the night-shift at a 24-hour salad bar..."

The customer's eyes will inevitably wander to the dunce-capped oval of the Atlantic Ocean Laundry;

"Before that, I put in five years on a hamburger assembly line..."

To the deep blue stain of the Damprag Linen Service;

"Before that, I was a canapé handler at a fancy hotel..."

Or to the pagoda-shaped monogram of the Mansoyl Towel and Apron Supply Co.

"And before that, I was in the Navy."

How does a half-apron from a glatt-kosher restaurant on Selah Avenue end up in the breakfast room of an Oarlock Falls Motel?

THE CUSTODIAN OF AN UNNAMED PARK, WEDGED BETWEEN EXIT NINE OF THE TARANTELLA PARKWAY AND THE RUSTY WATERS OF THE FERULE CANAL,

"THE WILD ASPIRIN": 10, 3:30 AND 9. "EYEBROW ALLEY": 11:30, 5 AND 10:30. "DEAD TO THE WORLD": 1:30, 7 AND 12:30.

PUTS IN AN EARLY-MORNING APPEARANCE.

THIS LOCATION DISSUADES FRESH-AIR LOVERS, POPSICLE-STICK COLLECTORS, WATER-FOUNTAIN ENTHUSIASTS AND SHORT-CUT SEEKERS.

HE UNCLOGS A FEW DRAINS OF FALLEN LEAVES AND STOLEN POCKETBOOKS,

IT WAS A POTTER'S FIELD RECLAIMED AND IMPROVED FOR THE BENEFIT OF THE LIVING.

UNLOCKS BOTH OF THE DOORS TO THE PUBLIC TOILET PAVILION

I TEAR OFF FIVE HUNDRED SHEETS A DAY TO MAKE IT LOOK BUSY.

WOMEN

—A STRUCTURE DONATED TO THE CITY BY THE MANUFACTURER OF A POPULAR OVER-THE-COUNTER DIARRHEA REMEDY—

"DEDICATED TO THE EPHEMERAL PLEASURES OF CHILDHOOD."

AND THEN GOES OFF TO SPEND THE DAY AT A TRIPLE-FEATURE MOVIE THEATER.

IT'S O.K., I SAW THE BEGINNING OF THE FIRST FILM YESTERDAY.

AT DUSK, HE RETURNS TO CLOSE UP THE PUBLIC TOILETS

AND SURVEY THIS QUIET SPOT WHERE NATURE CAN BE IGNORED.

I'LL CATCH THE END OF THE LAST FILM TOMORROW.

A HALF-PAGE TORN FROM LAST THURSDAY'S PAPER,

ANNOTATED IN RED WITH TICKS, ASTERISKS, CIRCLES AND LINES,

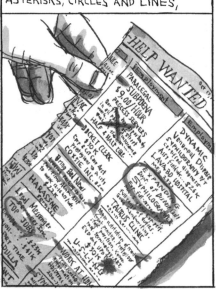

OFFERING EMPLOYMENT OPPORTU-NITIES IN THE FIELDS OF SUBPOENA SERVING TO SYPHILOGRAPHY—

BUT NOTHING FOR AN EXPERIENCED LIFEGUARD.

HOW CAN THE WHOLE STORY BE TOLD IN THE MINUSCULE PRINT OF THESE BRIEF PARAGRAPHS?

ONE MUST READ BETWEEN THE LINES AND COLUMNS, THE SMUDGES AND BROKEN TYPE,

TO FULLY COMPREHEND THIS MUTE CRY FOR HELP FROM THE CITY'S BUSINESS SECTOR—

A CRY WHICH NO ONE PERSON CAN ANSWER.

WITH GUARDED ENTHUSIASM, PREPARATIONS BEGIN FOR THE ANNUAL BANQUET OF THE LIVER AND KIDNEY DRAMATIC SOCIETY.

ON THIS SAME DARK DAY, FOR THE PAST EIGHT YEARS (ASIDE: YES, I TOO WAS A YOUNG MAN ONCE MYSELF!), I'VE COME TO YOU, A TOTAL STRANGER, WITH AN INVITATION— AND FOR EIGHT LONG YEARS, YOU'VE SPURNED MY EVERY ADVANCE.

A CATERER SAUTÉS A THOUSAND CALVES' ORGANS TO SERVE AS A SYMBOLIC APPETIZER.

LIVER FOR BILE, THE KIDNEYS FOR ADRENALINE.

A WORKER AT A CHAIR RENTAL COMPANY SCRAPES DRIED SOUP FROM THE PADDED SEATS OF FIVE HUNDRED FOLDING CHAIRS.

WHO KNOWS WHY THEY TREMBLE AT THESE AFFAIRS?

A RUN-DOWN HOTEL FUMIGATES ITS DISUSED BALLROOM.

A STAGE? WHO NEEDS A STAGE?

A SOCIETY MEMBER SELLS COMMEMORATIVE PAGES IN THE UPCOMING SOUVENIR PROGRAM BOOK.

TODAY I COME TO BESEECH YOU, IN THE NAME OF ALL THAT'S DECENT AND FAIR; IN THE NAME OF THE UNBORN GENERATIONS CERTAIN TO FOLLOW US THROUGH THIS VALE OF TEARS—I ASK YOU TO FORGET US (WHO ARE WE TO YOU?) AND INSTEAD, REMEMBER ONE OF YOUR OWN!

BUY A GOLD PAGE FOR FIVE HUNDRED DOLLARS TO COMMEMORATE A CARING PARENT OR GUARDIAN—NOW DECEASED—WHOSE VERY PRESENCE CAUSED YOU EMBARRASSMENT AS A CHILD.

OR, FOR TWO-HUNDRED AND FIFTY DOLLARS, A SILVER PAGE TO MEMORIALIZE A MOMENT OF BURNING ENVY FELT DURING YOUR ADOLESCENCE.

ON A BRONZE PAGE, FOR A HUNDRED TWENTY-FIVE, YOU CAN RECORD AN INSTANCE OF UNREQUITED LOVE —NO PROPER NAMES, PLEASE.

OR, MAY I PUT YOU DOWN AS A "WELL-WISHER" FOR JUST FIVE DOLLARS A LINE?

CAMBRIAN HOTEL

AS THEY HAVE EACH NIGHT AT SEVEN FOR THE PAST THIRTY YEARS,

YOU KNOW, NOEL KAPISH, THE FAMOUS DOUBLE-TALK ARTIST OF THE 1950s AND 60s.

THE DINNER CROWD ARRIVES AT NOEL KAPISH'S RESTAURANT AND SMOCKFRAIL HOUNDS.

ON ALL THE BIG TV SHOWS ...YOU MUST'VE SEEN HIM.

HE WAS JUST HERE BUT LEFT FOOTER GROUP OF FRIENDS AN A MEENY KAZUNA. THEY MACEY BLICK TOMATO, BUT I'M NOT SURE.

UNBEKNOWNST TO THEM ALL, THE CELEBRITY-RESTAURATEUR NOW SITS IN A CORRIDOR OF THE DEMENTIA WING OF A PRIVATE NURSING HOME.

I'D PREFER A BAKED POTATO WITH MY PUREED STEAK.

BUT HERE, EACH NIGHT AT DINNER TIME, HIS MENU, HIS DÉCOR AND HIS PERSONALITY ARE KEPT INTACT BY A DEVOTED STAFF.

HE JUST STEPPED LOUT BOTIL TWEE TWACK HENNA FINET.

SHOW THIS GENTLEMAN TO THE MINCE LOOM.

IN A WHIRLWIND OF ENFORCED GAIETY AND HEAVY FOOD, THE DYING MEMORIES OF THEIR ONCE-FAMOUS BOSS ARE MOMENTARILY REKINDLED.

WAWAZAT?

A CLUB SODA WITH LEMON!

IN THE CLATTER OF DIRTY DISHES, REGULAR CUSTOMERS IMAGINE THEY CAN HEAR HIS FAMILIAR VOICE,

WAWAZAT? WAWAZAT?

ON SLOW WEEKDAY NIGHTS, THE MAÎTRE D' WORRIES ABOUT THE FUTURE

CAN ONE REALLY BRIBE AN OBITUARY COLUMNIST? AND WHO'LL KEEP TRACK OF ALL THE DETAILS WHEN I RETIRE?

BUT FOR NOW, A FEW EXTRA BULBS IN THE ILLUMINATED OUTDOOR SIGN WILL SUFFICE.

COMPOSED EACH DAY UNDER THE NONCHALANT SUPERVISION OF COUNTLESS SECURITY GUARDS

NOV. 19, LEOPOLD PORTOLL VISITING THROATPIPE MINISTRIES, ROOM 1101, 2:07 P.M.

ARE THESE FASCINATING CHRONICLES OF THE COMMERCIAL LIFE OF THE CITY,

NOV. 19, M. JETSAMINA VISITING DR. PORIFERA, ROOM 917, 2:08 P.M.

HASTILY WRITTEN, IN TURN, BY THE PARTICIPANTS THEMSELVES,

NOV. 19, MOSES HUSSY VISITING THE ROMAN RENTAL LIBRARY, ROOM 51, 2:10 P.M.

NOV. 19, PADDY GATEAU VISITING THE NASAL INDEX CORP., ROOM 1019, 2:10 P.M.

THEY FORM AN EPIC TALE OF URGENT COMINGS AND GOINGS, STRANGE FAMILY NAMES AND MYSTERIOUS BUSINESS TRANSACTIONS CONDUCTED AT ALL HOURS OF THE DAY AND NIGHT.

NOV. 19, FLORA ESTRAY VISITING THE EXPULSION TRAVEL AGENCY, ROOM 772, 5:21 P.M.

NOV. 19, V. CUZO VISITING LAR-VAL FUNERAL ADVISORS, ROOM 1736, 5:22 P.M.

LOST MESSENGERS, RUTHLESS BUSINESSMEN AND INSATIABLE CUSTOMERS

NOV. 19, CAESAR BREGMA VISITING THE ALBUMEN SOCIETY, ROOM 801, 6:47 P.M.

MAKE BRIEF, YET TELLING, APPEARANCES ON ONE PAGE,

NOV. 19, J. KNIPL VISITING MENSTRUAL SYSTEMS, INC., ROOM 416, 7:00 P.M.

AND THEN TURN UP AGAIN NINETY PAGES (OR ONE MONTH) LATER UNDER SOMEWHAT ALTERED CIRCUMSTANCES;

PLEASE, PLEASE, LET ME DO THE TALKING.

STILL CAPABLE OF SIGNING THEIR OWN NAME

UM? ... J. KNIPL VISITING MENSTRUAL SYSTEMS, INC., ROOM 416, ... HMM?

BUT COMPLETELY UNAWARE OF THE DATE OR TIME OF THEIR LATEST APPEARANCE.

DEC. 19, I. DIMMER LEAVING KENOSIS MENSWEAR, ROOM 797, AT 3:28 P.M.

HMM?

THERE EXISTS NO MORE CONCLUSIVE EVIDENCE OF THE BRUTALITIES OF THE MODERN WORKPLACE

I TAKE IT OFF RIGHT AWAY AND HIDE IT IN MY POCKET.

THE CHABOUK CORP.
EMPLOYEE IDENTIFICATION
FRANCIS NOYSIA
MAR 1979
DATE OF ISSUE
SECURITY OFFICE

THAN THESE SMALL IDENTIFICATION PHOTOS WHICH HANG FROM THE POCKETS OF OFFICE WORKERS.

FROM BOY WONDER TO ENFEEBLED MIDDLE AGE IN FIFTEEN SHORT YEARS.

YOU'VE SEEN THEM IN THOSE ILLUMINATED FRAMES ON TAXI DASHBOARDS AND ON THE BADGES OF LICENSED STREET-PEDDLERS.

DAME

MINO ALZAK
1984
EXPIRES

AND IT'S UNDERSTANDABLE — THE EFFECTS OF THE INHUMANE WEATHER, THE LOW PAY...

FELIX CHAIN 1994

ALL BEEF

FRA
SOD

BUT SUCH DEVASTATION FROM SITTING AT A DESK FIVE DAYS A WEEK?

CAN THIS BE THE SAME MAN?

AT FIRST, I THOUGHT THAT IT WAS JUST A LOUSY PHOTOGRAPH.

CHABOUK CORP

LIKE THE HORRIFIC BEFORE-AND-AFTER ILLUSTRATIONS IN SOME MALEVOLENT PUBLIC HEALTH BULLETIN

BUT NOW, SECURITY GUARDS STOP ME; THINK I'M COVERING FOR A YOUNGER BROTHER WHO'S HOME WATCHING CARTOONS.

BOUK
CORPORATION

THE HEADLINE OF WHICH READS:

"AND THIS IS WHAT HAPPENS TO THE LUCKY ONES."

37 38 39 40 41 42 43 44

A CANCELED ORDER OVERHEARD IN A LOCAL RESTAURANT

ON SECOND THOUGHT, FORGET THE SALAMI AND EGGS. I'LL HAVE A LETTUCE AND TOMATO SANDWICH ON RYE INSTEAD.

PROVIDES MR. KNIPL WITH A TANTALIZING GLIMPSE OF ONE OTHER POSSIBLE COURSE OF EVENTS FOR THE STILL-YOUNG EVENING.

BY NOW, THE SMELL OF GARLIC AND FAT —A POWERFUL APHRODISIAC— WOULD FILL THE AIR.

THE PRESIDENT OF THE LOCAL CHAPTER OF AN INTERNATIONAL FOLK-DANCE CLUB ENTERS CARRYING A LARGE 78 R.P.M. PHONOGRAPH.

I WAS A PURIST, IN LOVE WITH THE IDEA OF AUTHENTIC DANCE FORMS.

HE SPOTS THE VERY MAN WHO, TWENTY-FIVE YEARS EARLIER, HE HAD EXPOSED FOR FALSIFYING THE STEPS OF A HABANERA.

FORGIVE ME. EVERYONE, FORGIVE ME. IT'S NOT TOO LATE.

IN A SWEEPING REVERSAL OF THE SOCIAL ORDER, HE BEGS THE WAITER TO SIT DOWN AND OFFERS TO EXPLAIN THE OBSCURE ETHNIC ORIGIN OF EACH DISH ON THE MENU.

ANYTHING YOU LIKE — AN APPETIZER, MAIN COURSE AND DESSERT.

A LATE EDITION OF THE DAILY PIGEON DECLARES ARTERIOSCLEROSIS TO BE A PSYCHOSOMATIC ILLNESS.

WHEN YOU UNDERSTAND THE TRUE HISTORY OF THIS FOOD, ITS FAT CONTENT BECOMES MEANINGLESS.

THE MILK OF HUMAN KINDNESS, CONDENSED INTO A DENTED SIXTEEN-OUNCE CAN, TURNS UP ON A SHELF OUTSIDE THE MEN'S ROOM.

THERE'S NO WAITING! EVERYTHING'S LAID OUT ON THE STEAM TABLE OF OUR COLLECTIVE UNCONSCIOUS.

NO WONDER HE SEEMS ANNOYED.

KILL THE SALAMI AND EGGS. GIVE ME A LETTUCE AND TOMATO ON RYE!

ARTHUR MAMMAL, A RETAILER OF SURGICAL SUPPLIES, HAS HIS MORNING COFFEE BY THE FRONT DOOR.

HE HOLDS HIS HAND LIKE THAT BECAUSE OF A HIATUS IN THE PORRIDGE VEIN OF HIS WRIST.

IN THE STRIDE AND POSTURE OF EACH PASSERBY,

SHE TREMBLES ON HER HEELS BECAUSE OF A CLEFT PELVIS.

HE CAN DISCERN THE EARLIEST SYMPTOMS OF THEIR PHYSICAL DECLINE.

THAT DISGUSTED LOOK IS DUE TO AN AFFLUX OF BLOOD TO THE LEFT SIDE OF HIS HEAD.

ON TUESDAYS, THE SALESMAN FROM GLEET SANITARY BANDAGE AND TRUSS COMPANY SHOWS UP

I SHOULD ORDER SOME MORE PLASTIC SHUNTS.

HONK HONK

WITH NEWS OF THE LATEST MEDICAL INNOVATIONS:

IT'S A PLUNGER —JUST LIKE THE ONE YOU USE IN YOUR TOILET— ONLY VERY, VERY SMALL.

YOUR PARTNER, FORTUS, AND THOUSANDS LIKE HIM WOULD BE ALIVE TODAY.

HOW A SIMPLE, ROUTINE PROCEDURE CAN NOW PREVENT SUCH DEATHS

SPARED THE BOILED-CABBAGE SERUM INJECTIONS, THE SODA-WATER BATHS AND COSTLY BRISKET OF BEEF GRAFTS— WHICH WERE ALL, IN THE END, FOR NAUGHT.

AND ALLOW ONE TO RESUME A NORMAL LIFE.

HE VEERS TOWARD THE CURB BECAUSE OF A CLONIC DISRUPTION IN THE MUSCLES OF HIS PORT CHESTER.

SKEERK

A KITCHEN DRAWER FILLED WITH FIVE YEARS' ACCUMULATION OF TAKE-OUT MENUS.

AT THE TABLE, A MAN TEETERS ON THE BRINK OF A DEEP HYPNOGOGIC TRANCE INDUCED BY THE FOLDING AND UNFOLDING OF ONE FAVORITE.

"SANJAK PALACE ... FREE DELIVERY."

HE INTONES THESE SAME WORDS FOR THE THOUSANDTH TIME,

I'D LIKE TO PLACE AN ORDER.

SMELLS THEIR KITCHEN ON A BUSY NIGHT IN THE FIBERS OF THE PAPER

NUMBER SEVENTEEN: YANKEE GOULASH WITH DROPPED EGGS ...

AND THEN HE SEES THAT FAMILIAR, AIR-CONDITIONED STOREFRONT IN WHICH TWO MEN DEBATE THE AESTHETICS OF A NEWLY INSTALLED GREASE TRAP.

AND ALSO NUMBER FORTY-THREE: KIPPERED HERRING PILAU WITH OYSTER PLANT.

ONE ALLUDES TO THE RUINS OF A SIXTEENTH-CENTURY ROYAL HAREM IN THEIR HOMELAND, THE OTHER TAKES AN ORDER.

A MARBLE CORRIDOR, BETWEEN BATHROOMS, WHERE A SULTAN ONCE SLIPPED AND DIED OF A BROKEN SKULL.

IS THAT IT?

HE'S DISCOVERED, LATE THAT NIGHT, BY HIS WIFE — ASLEEP ON THE COUCH, HIS PANTS SOILED, A GAUDY MENU IN HIS HAND.

YOU COULDN'T WAIT TILL I GOT HOME?

IN THE MORNING, SHE CLEANS OUT THE DRAWER AND TAPES AN ANGRY NOTICE TO THE FRONT VESTIBULE DOOR.

NO MENUS

EACH JANUARY, A SMALL NUMBER OF RADIATOR VIRTUOSI BEGIN THEIR SEASON OF SOLO CONCERTIZING.

BY THE WAY, I'M PLAYING HERE TONIGHT.

NEWSPAPER ADVERTISEMENTS ALERT A DISCRIMINATING PUBLIC TO THE TIME AND LOCATION OF THESE NIGHTLY EVENTS.

"FETOR MARACAS IN AN EVENING OF STEAM LULLABIES, APARTMENT 3-G, 235 VAYTIG AVENUE AT EIGHT."

FISSS

THE AUDIENCE IS USHERED INTO AN APARTMENT RENTED FOR THE EVENING.

I CHOSE THIS BUILDING FOR ITS BOILER—A 1949 "KYPHOS" WITH THE ORIGINAL TUBING—AND FOR THE ACOUSTIC WARMTH OF ITS TWO-BEDROOM APARTMENTS ON THE "G"-LINE.

THEY TAKE THEIR PLACE UPON FOLDING CHAIRS

EACH RADIATOR IN THE BUILDING CRIES WITH THE ANGER AND FRUSTRATION OF THE MIDDLE-CLASS TRAPPED ON THE TREADMILL OF CRUSHED EXPECTATIONS...

PLEASE...

AND SETTLE IN FOR A LONG PROGRAM OF KNOCKS AND HISSES,

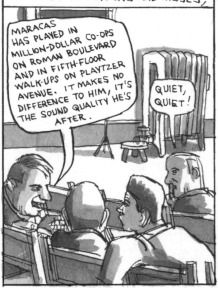

MARACAS HAS PLAYED IN MILLION-DOLLAR CO-OPS ON ROMAN BOULEVARD AND IN FIFTH-FLOOR WALK-UPS ON PLAYTZER AVENUE. IT MAKES NO DIFFERENCE TO HIM, IT'S THE SOUND QUALITY HE'S AFTER.

QUIET, QUIET!

FULLY AWARE OF THE ELEMENT OF CHANCE IN ALL SUCH ARTISTIC ENDEAVORS

THERE'S NOTHING COMING UP AND YOU HAVE A FULL HOUSE!

THAT'S BEYOND MY CONTROL; THE BOILER'S ON AN AUTOMATIC THERMOSTAT.

AND OF HOW A CAREER CAN BE RUINED IN A SINGLE NIGHT

LADIES AND GENTLEMEN, TONIGHT I MUST ASK FOR YOUR PATIENCE AND INDULGENCE.

BY THE ARRIVAL OF A FREAK WARM FRONT FROM THE GULF OF GOOD INTENTIONS.

WE'LL GIVE HIM TWENTY MINUTES, BUT THEN WE'RE LEAVING.

A PROCESSION OF TEN DUMPSTERS, EACH FILLED WITH A PAST YEAR'S ACCUMULATION

OF CITYWIDE PURCHASE ORDERS FOR STUFFED DERMA, OBITUARY NOTICES OF PROMINENT LABOR LEADERS AND DISCARDED PAPER CUPS FROM THE LOBBY WATER FOUNTAIN OF A CERTAIN DOWNTOWN EYE, EAR, NOSE AND THROAT HOSPITAL;

THE PROPORTIONS WITHIN THE AMALGAM MAY VARY, BUT THE TOTAL QUANTITY IS MIRACULOUSLY THE SAME EACH YEAR!

FOLLOWED BY A CORTEGE OF FRESH-EGG COURIERS — EACH WITH HIS HANDS FULL AND PANTS SPLIT;

FOLLOWED BY A LINE OF ICE-CREAM TRUCKS CHIMING IN UNISON THE NOTES OF AN ETERNAL JINGLE;

FOLLOWED BY HUNDREDS OF GROUPS REPRESENTING APARTMENT HOUSES THAT HAVE KEPT THE SAME STREET ADDRESS SINCE THEY WERE BUILT, MEN WHO CONTINUE TO DYE THEIR HAIR BLACK, LIQUOR STORES THAT HAVE NEVER CHANGED OWNERSHIP, ETC.

MR. KNIPL SITS IN A COFFEE SHOP ON A SIDE STREET, JUST OFF THE PARADE ROUTE.

IT'S THE SAME EVERY YEAR — THE STASIS DAY PARADE — AND I ALWAYS FORGET TO STAY OUT OF MIDTOWN.

A WEARY MARCHER COMES IN TO REST.

ISN'T IT ENOUGH I DO THIS FOR A LIVING FIVE DAYS A WEEK...

HIS PANTS ARE SPLIT.

I HAVE TO MAKE A PUBLIC SHOW OF UNITY ON MY DAY OFF?

LET SOMEBODY ELSE TELL HIM.

The Stasis Day Parade 69

MR. KNIPL NOTICES YET ANOTHER MAN IN THE STREET WITH A SMALL TRANSISTOR RADIO PRESSED TO HIS EAR.

A BIG GAME? A NEW WAR?

A NATURAL DISASTER? ... WHAT'S HAPPENING?

WAIT. QUIET! I'M TRYING TO HEAR!

REESE HAROUNI, THE WORLD CHAMPION PUDDLE-JUMPER, LOST A GALOSH DURING COMPETITION IN A THUNDERSTORM ON THE COAST OF CISTERNA. THOUSANDS OF INNOCENT SPECTATORS WERE SOAKED TO THE BONE, HUNDREDS OF HAIR-DOS WERE RUINED AND THE PRICE OF A FOLDING PLASTIC RAIN BONNET SOARED TO TWO DOLLARS ON THE BLACKMARKET. UMBRELLA TROOPS WERE SENT IN TO RECOVER THE LOST SHOE BUT MET RESISTANCE FROM LOCAL ZEALOTS FOR WHOM THE PUDDLE HAS HISTORICAL AND RELIGIOUS SIGNIFICANCE.

THEY SEEM SO CALM, MERE IDLERS, BUT IN FACT, THESE MEN ARE THE BULWARKS OF ALL HUMAN DECENCY. THEY ACT AS BUFFERS AGAINST THE HORRIFIC ONSLAUGHT OF DAILY NEWS. WE SIT IN THE SUN AND CONSIDER OUR MORAL OPTIONS WHILE THEY GO THROUGH THREE SETS OF BATTERIES IN A WEEK!

DURING THESE INTERNATIONAL CRISES, THEY LIVE THEIR LIVES WITH ONLY ONE HAND FREE ...

A "ROCK OF AGES" BAR, PLEASE.

TO COUNT CHANGE,

HAROUNI CAN BREAK THE WORLD RECORD THIS AFTERNOON ONLY IF IT STOPS RAINING.

TO ADJUST THEIR RADIO,

THE AERIAL BOMBARDMENT OF CISTERNA HAS BEEN POSTPONED DUE TO POOR VISIBILITY ...

A "ROCK OF AGES" BAR?

KASBAH NEWS
CANDY SODA

AND TO EAT CANDY BARS.

I DON'T UNDERSTAND. DID HE LOSE A SHOE, A GALOSH OR BOTH?

WE DON'T KNOW. IT'S IN THE PUDDLE AND THEY WON'T LET ANYONE LOOK.

A NUMBER OF DRAMATISTS HAVE TURNED TO THE SIGHTSEEING TOUR BUS AS A UNIQUE AND AFFORDABLE METHOD OF REALIZING A THEATRICAL SPECTACLE IN THE MIDST OF A DEPRESSED ECONOMY.

THEY'RE OTHERWISE IDLE AT NIGHT AND THEY SEAT FIFTY-FIVE!

CIMAX TOURS

EACH EVENING AT EIGHT, AT AN ADVERTISED LOCATION, ONE CAN CATCH THE SHOW OF THEIR CHOICE.

"THE TEXTBOOK EXILE," FROM THE CORNER OF SCYTHE AND TIGRIS AT 8 P.M. "AH, THALAMUS!," FROM PORTERHOUSE SQ. AT 8 P.M. "AN INFORMAL FLU," FROM IN FRONT OF THE LUNAR HOTEL AT 8 P.M. ...

AH, THALAMUS! by PONTI DUEL

THROUGH THE USE OF A POWERFUL DIRECTIONAL SPOTLIGHT, THE ENTIRE CITY IS REDUCED TO A SERIES OF SCENIC TABLEAUX AT THE DISPOSAL OF THE AUTHOR'S IMAGINATION.

AS WE APPROACH THIS INTERSECTION, I ASK YOU TO LOOK TO YOUR RIGHT... WE SEE A 24-HOUR SALAD BAR WHERE NIGHT WORKERS GO TO LOSE THEMSELVES IN THE REFRIGERATED MISCELLANY OF A CANOPIED BANQUET TABLE.

NOBLE PRICE FOOD FARM

TEXTBOOK EXILE

WHILE MOST PRODUCTIONS HAVE ADOPTED THE CLASSIC TOUR GUIDE'S PATTER-AND-POINT TECHNIQUE — JUST RAISED TO NEW HEIGHTS OF POETIC DICTION —

NOW, IF YOU CAN, PLEASE LOOK TO YOUR LEFT. THERE, JUST MOVING INTO OUR SPOTLIGHT, IS A COMMON DUMPSTER FILLED TO THE BRIM WITH THE REMAINS OF A FAILED BUSINESS...

SOME PRODUCTIONS EMPLOY ACTORS STRATEGICALLY PLANTED ON STREET CORNERS, IN THE WINDOWS OF GROUND-FLOOR APARTMENTS

AND HERE IS CARLOS MUTUAL, A PUBLIC-ADDRESS SYSTEMS ANALYST SUFFERING FROM TONSILLITIS...

OR AT PUBLIC BUS STOPS, AS A MEANS OF ADVANCING THEIR NARRATIVE SCHEME.

HIS FRIEND, SYLVAN, HAS BEEN WAITING FOR AN ANNOUNCEMENT ALL DAY...

THE TEXTBOOK EXILE by Matthias Fistula

BUS STOP

SEVERAL CRITICS, STRICKEN BY THE MOTION SICKNESS ASSOCIATED WITH BUS TRAVEL, HAVE BEEN UNFAIR IN THEIR APPRAISAL OF THESE WORKS.

I HAD TO LEAVE AT INTERMISSION.

DONUT

THIS RELATIVELY NEW, HYBRID FORM OF THEATER IS NATURALLY SUBJECT TO THE EXCESSES AND EXUBERANCE OF YOUTH.

THAT'S IT. SHOW'S OVER. GOOD NIGHT!

BUT HOW CAN WE GET A TAXI HERE IN THE MIDDLE OF NOWHERE?

TO THE DISMAY OF THE PRODUCERS, WRITERS AND ACTORS IN THE WORLD OF EXCURSIONIST DRAMA,

IT'S LIKE GOING TO THE THEATER TO WATCH THE CURTAIN GO UP AND DOWN!

THE TEXTBOOK EXILE by Matthias Firkata

THE AUDIENCE HAS, OF LATE, BEGUN TO TURN ITS ATTENTIONS TO THE PERFORMANCE OF THE BUS DRIVER,

THEY'RE DOING "THE TEXTBOOK EXILE" AGAIN TONIGHT.

I KNOW, BUT WHO'S AT THE WHEEL?

THE PLAY, THESE AFICIONADOS CLAIM, IS MERELY AN OPPORTUNITY FOR THE VIRTUOSO DISPLAY OF MODERN MOTOR-COACH HANDLING.

CRISSUM.

CRISSUM? I UNDERSTAND THAT HE NOW USES AN AIR-FLOW SEAT PAD.

OTHERS SEE THE INDIVIDUAL DRIVER'S BRAKING, STEERING AND REGULATION OF THE PNEUMATIC SYSTEM, DURING THE COURSE OF AN EVENING, AS A SUBTEXT TO THE PLAY—

"TO YOUR RIGHT, WE SEE A 24-HOUR SALAD BAR WHERE NIGHT WORKERS GO TO LOSE THEMSELVES..."

FEEL HOW HE CREEPS UP ON THE LIGHT?

MAT TOURS

THE MEANING OF WHICH IS BEST UNDERSTOOD WITH CLOSED EYES,

"...IN THE REFRIGERATED MISCELLANY OF A CANOPIED BANQUET TABLE."

HIS DRIVING'S MEANT TO MAKE YOU SICK.

MALE AND FEMALE PASSENGERS ALIKE HAVE BEEN ESPECIALLY TAKEN WITH THE TECHNIQUE OF A CERTAIN BAPTISTE PASCHAL.

UNTIL RECENTLY, HE WAS AN UNEMPLOYED CITY BUS DRIVER.

PRODUCERS FEAR THAT THIS UNDUE ATTENTION WILL ALLOW DRIVERS, LIKE MR. PASCHAL, TO DEMAND HIGHER FEES FOR THEIR SERVICES,

TO GO NORTH OF THE MILDEW BRIDGE, I WANT AN EXTRA TWENTY-FIVE DOLLARS.

THUS PLACING ECONOMIC CONSTRAINTS UPON THE IMAGINATION OF THE PLAYWRIGHT.

WE'LL HAVE HIM MAKE A U-TURN JUST BEFORE THE BRIDGE— THE AUDIENCE'LL GO CRAZY!

BY SEVEN O'CLOCK THERE'S A TICKET LINE OUTSIDE OF TRAMPOLINE HALL FOR THE NIGHTLY IMPROMPTU LECTURE BY HAROLD ALMS.

"THE PSYCHOGENESIS OF A CLUB SANDWICH," "KNICKKNACKS IN THE POST-INDUSTRIAL AGE," "IS SANTA CLAUS A JEW?"...

IN THE HOUR BEFORE HIS APPEARANCE, THIS RENOWNED SPEAKER SITS AT HIS DRESSING ROOM WINDOW INTENT ON SENSING NOTHING MORE THAN THE TEMPERATURE AND BAROMETRIC PRESSURE OF THE STREET OUTSIDE.

"PROPHECY AND PASTEURISM," "THE GLORIFICATION OF THE KIDNEY," "IMITATIONS OF LAUGHTER IN THE 20TH CENTURY"...

THE PUBLIC IS ONLY DIMLY AWARE OF THE EXTRAORDINARY MEASURES TAKEN BY MR. ALMS TO PREVENT HIMSELF FROM PREMEDITATING THE EVENING'S LECTURE.

AND TONIGHT?

WHO KNOWS? HE DOESN'T KNOW HIMSELF UNTIL THE LAST MINUTE.

HE LIVES IN A FURNISHED SINGLE ROOM, BEREFT OF ALL PERSONAL ASSOCIATIONS.

IS THAT MY TOOTHBRUSH?!

TWO RADIOS, TUNED TO DIFFERENT STATIONS, SERVE AS A CONSTANT SOURCE OF DISTRACTION.

...IN THE FIRST ACT OF TONIGHT'S OPERA, WE HEAR THE YOUNG TENOR, HECTOR GLANZ, SINGING THE ARIA "SPECIE D'INSETTO"

COMING INTO THE STRETCH, IT'S EUPHORIA... EUPHORIA BY A NOSE!

HIS BOOKCASE IS EMPTIED EACH NIGHT WITH THE GARBAGE AND REFILLED IN THE MORNING BY A DELIVERY BOY FROM THE LOCAL BRANCH OF A NATIONAL BOOKSTORE CHAIN.

A RANDOM SAMPLING OF REMAINDERED BEST-SELLERS.

HIS MEALS ARE TAKEN EXCLUSIVELY IN BUSY COFFEE-SHOPS WHERE HE CAN LOSE HIMSELF IN THE DIN OF HEAVY-GAUGE CHINA.

HE APPROACHES THE PODIUM WITHOUT A THOUGHT IN HIS HEAD, TURNS OFF THE LAMP, AND BEGINS.

MY LECTURE TONIGHT IS ENTITLED...

AFTER FORTY YEARS OF SELLING WHOLE-SALE INDUSTRIAL DEODORIZING SUPPLIES, ONE ESTABLISHMENT IS FORCED TO OPEN ITS DOORS TO THE PUBLIC.

IN THE LINGO OF THE TRADE, A SALESMAN EXPLAINS WHY THEIR LARGE INSTITUTIONAL BUYERS HAVE GONE ELSEWHERE.

WHO WANTS TO STAND DOWNWIND OF THE LEAGUE O' NATIONS EVERY TIME SOME FRESHMAN WITH A BLADDER INFECTION PULLS A NEBUCHADNEZZAR?

HE AND HIS ASSOCIATES HAVE NO PATIENCE FOR THE OFF-THE-STREET TRADE WITH ITS PETTY CONCERNS AND MINIMUM ORDERS.

WHEN I REMOVE MY HAT THERE'S A CERTAIN SMELL, BUT ONLY FOR A MOMENT.

IT'S JUST FOR MY HUSBAND AND MYSELF!

IN FACT, THEY SUSPECT THAT THESE ARE THE VERY SAME PEOPLE WHO URINATE IN THE HALLWAYS OF SMALL APARTMENT BUILDINGS,

I'D SELL THEM A YEAR'S SUPPLY OF NAPHTALENE AIR FRESHENERS...

IMPREGNATE THE UPHOLSTERY OF HOTEL LOBBY FURNITURE WITH THE SCENT OF HAIR CREAM AND COLOGNE,

A COMPUTER-CONTROLLED MINT ATOMIZER...

AND RIDE WITH SANDWICHES FROM HOME IN THE ELEVATORS OF MODERN OFFICE BUILDINGS,

SIXTY POUNDS OF BAY RUM SWEEPING COMPOUND!

THEY COME TO GAZE IN MOCK ASTONISHMENT AT EQUIPMENT AND CHEMICAL PREPARATIONS DESIGNED TO MASK ODORS OF A MAGNITUDE THEY'VE NEVER KNOWN.

IMAGINE THE SMELL OF A CHANGE PURSE MULTIPLIED A HUNDRED THOUSAND TIMES.

ONE CUSTOMER IS SENT ON HIS WAY WITH A TEN-GALLON DRUM OF ANTI-PERSPIRANT.

WHILE DESCENDING THE BACK STAIRWAY OF HIS APARTMENT BUILDING, MR. KNIPL HAS SUDDENLY REVEALED TO HIM AN UNOBSTRUCTED VIEW INTO A "G"-LINE KITCHEN.

THAT'S MR. MIGNON!

A MAN, STRUCK BY THE REALIZATION THAT EVERYTHING IN HIS REFRIGERATOR IS AN IMITATION OR MOCK VERSION OF SOME ONCE "REAL" PRODUCT, WEEPS INTO A PAPER TOWEL.

SOY CREAM CHEESE, BEEF BACON, MAN-MADE EGGS, NON-DAIRY CREAMER, VEGETARIAN CHICKEN FAT...

THE POOR GUY—SPENDS ALL DAY IN THE IMPORT-EXPORT BUSINESS AND THEN COMES HOME TO THIS!

HIS SON, A PRODUCT OF ARTIFICIAL INSEMINATION, STANDS IN THE LOBBY WITH A STRANGE MAN.

THAT'S A TOUPEE IF I EVER SAW ONE.

HIS WIFE WAITS OUTSIDE IN A PARKED CAR.

FAKE FUR AND FALSE EYELASHES.

MR. KNIPL CONFIDES IN THE BUILDING'S SUPERINTENDENT

THE POOR MAN'S ALL ALONE UP THERE, TERRIBLY DISTRAUGHT... WHAT IS HIS FAMILY DOING?

YOU'RE RIGHT, ABSOLUTELY RIGHT.

AT LEAST THEY COULD TAKE HIM OUT FOR A GOOD MEAL.

AND MINUTES LATER, A DEAL IS CONSUMMATED.

I NEVER SAW SUCH A REACTION.

THEY'RE GENUINE GLYCERIN TEARDROPS IMPORTED FROM FRANCE.

AND HE'S JUST AN UPSTAIRS NEIGHBOR... A MERE ACQUAINTANCE.

I'M CONVINCED. PUT ME DOWN FOR SIX CASES.

ON THE THIRTY-SIXTH FLOOR OF THE TRIBULATION TOWER, IN THE OFFICE OF THE Y. KANCHEW CO.,

THERE SITS ON A BROOM CLOSET SHELF A RUSTY AND FORGOTTEN CAN OF "BECALM" BRAND AEROSOL SPRAY.

AT THE SUGGESTION OF CERTAIN POST-WAR EFFICIENCY EXPERTS, A THIN COAT OF THIS MILD GLUE WAS SPRAYED EACH NIGHT ON EVERY OFFICE CHAIR.

ACCORDING TO THEIR STATISTICS, THIS SIMPLE EXPEDIENT WOULD REDUCE COFFEE-BREAK, REST-ROOM AND IDLE WANDERING TIME BY FOUR-TENTHS OF A PERCENT DURING AN AVERAGE DAY.

IN TIME, IT WAS DISCOVERED THAT THIS SAME GLUE ACCUMULATED IN THE FORM OF A TACKY FILM UPON THE SEATS OF TROUSERS AND SKIRTS OF CLERKS AND SECRETARIES BETWEEN VISITS TO THE LAUNDRY.

AS A RESULT, THEY'D FIND THEMSELVES, TOWARD THE END OF EACH WEEK, STUCK IN VARIOUS UNPRODUCTIVE SITUATIONS:

A MISSED BUS-STOP ON THE WAY TO WORK, A HALF-HOUR SPENT OVER A BAKED APPLE IN A CAFETERIA AT LUNCH TIME, TWENTY MINUTES PERCHED ON A COLLEAGUE'S DESK WITH A WINDOW VIEW.

THE MAN-HOURS THUS LOST FAR OUTWEIGHED THE BENEFITS CLAIMED BY EVEN THE MOST ARDENT PROPONENT OF THIS MODERN FORM OF TRANQUILIZER.

THE HIGHLIGHT OF THIS YEAR'S "NATIONAL WOE AND WHOLESALE LAMENTATION SHOW" IS AN ELECTRIC EYE DESIGNED TO AUTOMATI- CALLY SHED A PREDETERMINED NUMBER OF TEARS WHEN AN INDIVIDUAL OR SITUATION OF SUFFICIENT SADNESS PASSES BEFORE IT.

THIS GLASS EYE TAKES IN THE MORNING THRONG OF VISITORS — AND REMAINS DRY.

THEN, EVERY HOUR ON THE HALF HOUR, A CERTIFIABLY SAD SUBJECT IS BROUGHT TO THE EXHIBITION HALL AND MARCHED BEFORE THE SENSITIVE EYE.

TO THE ASTONISHMENT OF THE GATHERED CROWD, A DAMP SPOT APPEARS ON THE FLOOR.

JUST BEFORE NOON, A JANITOR WITH COLITIS AND A BAD KNEE UNINTENTIONALLY TRIGGERS THE ELECTRIC EYE.

ONCE SET IN MOTION, THIS DELICATE ELECTRONIC INSTRUMENT BEGINS TO SENSE A CAUSE FOR TEARS IN EACH PASSERBY.

THE AFTERNOON CROWD TRACKS SYNTHETIC TEAR-FLUID THROUGH THE EXHIBITION HALL.

THAT EVENING, THE EXHIBIT IS TEMPO- RARILY WITHDRAWN FOR THE PURPOSE OF MAKING ADJUSTMENTS TO THE MACHINE'S VARIABLE TEAR-DUCT AND HIGH-SPEED MELANCHOLY SENSORS.

THE INVENTOR GUSTAVE VINT TAKES HIS PROTOTYPE OF A NEW-STYLE BRIEFCASE OUT FOR A TRIAL RUN.

I DON'T KNOW YET WHAT TO CALL IT, BUT A NAME WILL COME TO ME EVENTUALLY.

WHEN PLACED ON THE GROUND, IT INSTANTLY SPRINGS OPEN INTO THE FORM OF A STANDARD WASTEPAPER BASKET

ITS OWN WEIGHT RELEASES A SMALL INTERNAL CATCH.

AND THEN, WHEN PICKED UP BY ITS HANDLE, COLLAPSES BACK INTO THE SHAPE OF A BRIEFCASE.

IT'S ALL BASED UPON THE FACT THAT ONE MAN'S WASH-OUT IS ANOTHER MAN'S LUCKY BREAK.

THIS SIMPLE INVENTION IS MEANT TO INCREASE THE FLOW OF MERCANTILE ENERGY FROM ONE CORNER OF THE CITY TO ANOTHER BY TENFOLD.

HERE, LOOK WHAT I'VE PICKED UP IN JUST FIVE MINUTES: AN EXPIRED TRANSFER FOR THE GALLSTONE AVENUE BUS; A HALF-PRICE COUPON FOR VEGETARIAN HAIR IMPLANTS; AND A MOTHER-OF-PEARL-FINISH BUSINESS CARD WITH A CHANGE OF ADDRESS WRITTEN IN BY HAND - DR. HARMEL LOATY, TOMATO HERRING SPECIALIST!

A WHOLESALER OF CRADLE-CAP REMEDIES WILLINGLY DISCARDS A HOPELESS LEAD:

THESE BASTARDS THINK I'M DOING THIS AS A HOBBY FOR TWENTY YEARS.

THAT'S THE WAY IT GOES. PASS IT ALONG, BROTHER.

A NAME AND ADDRESS WHICH, IN THE HANDS OF A PROMOTER OF NOVELTY MACARONI, PRESENTS A GOLDEN OPPORTUNITY.

IT'S A STEP IN THE RIGHT DIRECTION - TO SPREAD THE FRUITS OF ECONOMIC SUCCESS MORE EVENLY AMONG THOSE INVOLVED...

WITH THIS ENCOURAGEMENT, THE INVENTOR RETURNS TO THE QUIET SANCTUARY OF HIS FURNISHED ROOM,

BUT I ADMIT, THERE ARE STILL SOME BUGS TO BE WORKED OUT.

ROOM TO LET

NO LOITER

WHERE, IN THE MIDDLE OF THE NIGHT, HE'S AWAKENED BY THE GRINDING SCREAM OF A COMMERCIAL GARBAGE TRUCK.

EUREKA!

PIZZA
PYLORUS

SYLVAN CARTING

THE GREAT-GRANDDAUGHTER OF A NATIONALLY KNOWN TURN-OF-THE-CENTURY SAUSAGE MANUFACTURER

THEY SOLD THE FAMILY NAME TWENTY YEARS AGO TO SOME BIG JUNK-FOOD CONGLOMERATE.

ASKS HER PROSPECTIVE BOY-FRIENDS TO PROVE THEIR WORTH

ARE YOU FAMILIAR WITH BALAAM'S DELICATESSEN ON LIKEUR AVENUE?

BY STEALING FOR HER A JAR OF PICKLED TOMATOES AND RED PEPPERS FROM THE WINDOW OF A LOCAL DELICATESSEN OR SANDWICH SHOP.

THEY'VE BEEN SITTING THERE UNTOUCHED FOR SEVENTEEN YEARS — NOBODY'LL EVEN NOTICE.

ANYTHING FOR CELIA.

ARRAYED IN SINGLE FILE OR STACKED IN PYRAMIDAL FORM, THESE JARS SERVE AS A TRADITIONAL SHOW OF BOUNTY —

THE LIRA SANDWICH CHALET ON NOETIC STREET?

ANYTHING FOR CELIA

A HINT OF THE GENEROUS HANDLING OF FOOD WITHIN.

PELLAGRA'S LUNCH BOX ON SIKROOM STREET?

ANYTHING FOR CELIA.

AS THE BRINE BECOMES CLOUDY WITH AGE, THE TRANSLUCENT TOMATOES RISE HOPEFULLY TO THE UPENDED GLASS BOTTOM OF EACH JAR.

A DELICATE CIRCLE, FREE OF SOOT, IS THE ONLY EVIDENCE OF MY CRIME.

THESE SAME OBJECTS, WHICH FOR YEARS PIQUED THE APPETITES OF CASUAL PASSERSBY,

IT'S ME, ELEAZAR.

NOW EXERCISE A STRANGE POWER OVER ONE RECUMBENT YOUNG WOMAN.

I HOPE YOU'RE NOT ALONE.

WHAT SEEMS AT FIRST GLANCE TO BE JUST ANOTHER POOR MAN SCROUNGING FOR CIGARETTE BUTTS IN THE STREET

AH! A "LUCKY STAR" WITH "PRINCESS SCARLATINA'S SUMMER BLUSH NO. 3."

IS IN ACTUALITY A PASSIONATE CONNOISSEUR IN PURSUIT OF A RARE AND ELUSIVE QUARRY.

BUT ONLY THOSE STAINED BY LIPSTICK?

I WAS ORIGINALLY ATTRACTED TO LIP-STICK-KISSED COFFEE CUPS, BUT THAT BECAME AN EXPENSIVE PROPOSITION.

EACH SPECIMEN IS UNIQUE UNTO ITSELF — A SYNTHESIS OF THE NATURAL AND MAN-MADE WORLDS.

YOU HAVE TO KNOW WHERE TO LOOK. HERE, IN FRONT OF THE PHYLUM INSURANCE COMPANY, JUST AFTER LUNCH, THE SIDEWALK'S THICK WITH THEM. IT'S JUST A MATTER OF GETTING THERE FIRST, BEFORE THE NEXT GUY.

SHOULD A QUESTION OF ATTRIBUTION ARISE, OTHER IMPARTIAL EXPERTS ARE CALLED UPON FOR ADVICE.

THAT'S A "MOUNT EVEREST MENTHOL" TINGED WITH "CRIMSON CHERRY FOREVER". IF YOU DON'T BELIEVE ME, LOOK AT THE CHART YOURSELF.

IT'S LIKE STAMP COLLECTING IN THAT SOMEONE ELSE DOES THE LICKING.

UNDERLYING THIS SOPHISTICATED OUTDOOR HOBBY IS A MORBID FETISHISTIC IMPULSE—

I FIGURE THAT HALF OF MY COLLECTION OF "MAHARAJAH FILTERS" WITH DEEP-RED STAINS FROM THE 1950s CAME FROM THE LIPS OF WOMEN WHO ARE NOW DEAD.

AN IMPULSE CONDITIONED BY A BURNING ENVY OF ONE'S FELLOW MAN,

SOME OF THESE GUYS APPROACH THE SMOKER DIRECTLY AND MAKE ARRANGEMENTS TO HAVE THE BUTT SET ASIDE FOR THEM WHEN THE CIGARETTE'S FINISHED.

BASED UPON A PERVERSE AESTHETIC DELIGHT IN WHAT ONE CAN NEVER REALLY KNOW—

BUT WHAT BECOMES OF THAT NATURAL GESTURE OF RELINQUISHMENT — THE UNSEEN FLICK OF THE WRIST?

ALL SUFFUSED WITH A PROFOUND SENSE OF UTTER FUTILITY.

YOU MIGHT AS WELL PUT ON LIPSTICK AND SMOKE THE CIGARETTE YOURSELF.

A NARROW STREET AT LUNCH TIME IN THE RAIN, AS SEEN FROM THE SAFETY OF A LUNCHEONETTE BOOTH.

THERE IS A TREMENDOUS POTENTIAL FOR DISASTER HERE. EACH UMBRELLA HAS EIGHT RIBS, AND MOST PEDESTRIANS STILL HAVE TWO EYES.

I HAD JUST COME UP OUT OF THE SUBWAY, WHEN IT STARTED TO RAIN. I STOPPED FOR A MINUTE IN FRONT OF THE NEWSSTAND TO READ THE HEADLINES, SEE WHAT'S GOING ON, AND THE NEXT THING I KNOW, SOMEONE GETS ME RIGHT HERE—ONE INCH LOWER AND IT WOULD HAVE BEEN SERIOUS.

PLEASE, PLEASE....

ON A DAY LIKE THIS, THE EMERGENCY ROOMS ARE FILLED WITH INNOCENT PEOPLE WHO HAVE ACTUALLY BEEN POKED IN THE EYE. THEIR SIGHT HAS BEEN PERMANENTLY DAMAGED. I HAVE NO SYMPATHY TO SPARE FOR SOMEONE LIKE YOU WHO'S HAD A LITTLE FRIGHT—A CLOSE CALL.

TONIGHT, OR WHENEVER THE RAIN STOPS, I GO WITH A GROUP OF LIKE-MINDED INDIVIDUALS TO THE CLAMSHELL HOSPITAL TO OFFER MY CONDOLENCES TO THE FAMILIES OF THE INJURED. COME WITH US TONIGHT. BE A MAN—IT'S A HEART-BREAKING SIGHT BUT IT WILL DO YOU GOOD TO SEE.

... TO MEASURE WITH YOUR OWN EYES THE NARROW CHASM BETWEEN "ALMOST" AND "WHAT IS."

BUT EVEN HERE YOU'LL FIND MALINGERERS, SYMPATHY SEEKERS—PEOPLE, WITH SLIGHTLY BRUISED SCLERAS OR SUPERFICIAL SCRATCHES ON THEIR CORNEA, SITTING IN HOSPITAL BEDS ON THE PHONE WITH THEIR LAWYERS TRYING TO MAKE A LITTLE MONEY. LET'S GO...

FOLLOW ME, THEY HAVE ANOTHER ROOM BACK HERE FOR THE OVERFLOW... BUT IT'S A SLOW NIGHT.

LOOK, THESE THINGS CAN'T BE ARRANGED FOR YOUR EDIFICATION. COME SEE ME TOMORROW AT THE LUNCHEONETTE, SAME TIME, SAME BOOTH—IT'S SUPPOSED TO RAIN.

A CRIME IS COMMITTED

BE ON THE LOOKOUT FOR A WHITE MALE, AGE FORTY, LAST SEEN WEARING A DOUBLE-BREASTED STEVEDORE-STYLE LOAFING SUIT.

A WITNESS COMES FORWARD

HIS SUIT WAS MADE OF EMERALD GREEN BURLAP WITH FLESH-COLORED-NYLON KNEE AND ELBOW PATCHES. I CAN NEVER FORGET IT.

AND THE WEB OF GUILT SPREADS—

WHAT DID HE DO?

WHO KNOWS, WHO CARES. HE'S JUST A DUPE, WE'RE AFTER THE BIG BOYS.

TO A CLOTHING STORE ON SLIPKNOT AVENUE,

YES, WE CARRY A FULL LINE OF LOAFING SUITS AND IDLE-WEAR, BUT YOU HAVE TO BE MORE SPECIFIC— DID IT HAVE A MOCK DRY-CLEANING TICKET STAPLED TO ITS HEM? DID IT HAVE PRE-STAINED ARMPITS? A SET OF GILDED PURSE STRINGS HANGING FROM EACH SIDE?

I DON'T KNOW. YOU TELL ME WHAT'S SELLING.

TO A WHOLESALER OF MEN'S APPAREL,

VERY POPULAR AMONG MIDDLE-CLASS EXHIBITIONISTS AND WEEKEND JUJITSUISTS. IT'S IMPOSSIBLE TO SIT STILL AND CONCENTRATE IN SUCH A GET-UP. IT HAS SIX ZIPPERS AND A VELCRO-PADLOCKED COLLAR— HE'D BLEND RIGHT IN.

CALLOUS YOUTH MENSWEAR

TO A MANUFACTURING PLANT SIX THOUSAND MILES AWAY,

ARE YOU IMPLYING THAT ONE OF OUR GARMENTS, WORN BY THIS ALREADY SICK INDIVIDUAL, INCITED HIM TO DO WHAT HE DID? DON'T BE SILLY. WE SELL HUNDREDS OF THOUSANDS OF LOAFING SUITS TO MEN IN ALL WALKS OF LIFE— THE FABRIC OF SOCIETY WOULD BE SHOT THROUGH WITH DISHONESTY AND VICE.

SIZE 16

TO A DESIGNER'S STUDIO IN A RENOVATED DOCKSIDE WAREHOUSE,

SOMETIMES, AN OUTFIT IN THE LATEST STYLE GIVES AN OTHERWISE TIMID SOUL THE LICENSE TO TRANSGRESS THE BOUNDS OF CIVIL DECENCY. YES, IN THAT CASE, I'M GUILTY. TAKE ME AWAY.

TO A WOMAN BUYING A BIRTHDAY PRESENT FOR HER GRANDCHILD.

WE HAVE THESE DOUBLE-BREASTED STEVEDORE-STYLE LOAFING SUITS IN SIZES EIGHTEEN MONTHS TO THREE YEARS.

Li'l Idler dept.

JUST BEYOND THE HOTEL GATES, CONFIRMED BACHELORS TEND THE ROWS OF PEPPERMINT PLANTS USED FOR FLAVORING.

I WAS DIGESTING MY LUNCH.

YOU DIDN'T COME HERE TO SIT ON THE PORCH ALL DAY—DID YOU?

ON THE FOOTHILL SLOPES OF MOUNT KYAN STAND THE GROVES OF MIDGET BIRCH TREES WHICH YIELD THE PERFECTLY FORMED SPLINTS OF FINE-GRAINED WOOD FOUND IN THE BEST RESTAURANTS.

THE SPECIAL TONIGHT IS STUFFED CABBAGE.

DON'T WORRY, THE SECOND SITTING IS AT EIGHT AND IT'LL STILL BE LIGHT OUT.

HERE, WHERE THE RIVER MINTZ MEETS THE MOHLAR PASS, TOURISTS COME TO ENJOY THE PLEASURES OF TOOTHPICKING.

OUR PICKS ARE ALL SPLAYED AND WE'RE MILES FROM THE HOTEL.

RIGHT NOW THEY'RE SERVING DESSERT.

AT RUSTIC DINING-ROOM TABLES, RETIRED DENTURE WEARERS SIT ALONGSIDE GAP-TOOTHED YOUTHS ON THEIR SPRING VACATION.

WE BRING OUR OWN HOLLOW-CORE STAINLESS STEEL PICKS...

IN A MONOGRAMMED LEATHER VEST-POCKET SHEATH.

BETWEEN MEALS OF CORN ON THE COB, BEEFSTEAK AND OTHER FIBROUS FOODS,

GIVE ME A ROUND, MINT-FLAVORED WOODEN PICK IN A SANITARY PAPER WRAPPER ANY DAY.

FLAT, ROUND, WHO CARES?

THEY HIKE THE MOUNTAIN PATHS EQUIPPED WITH NOTHING MORE THAN A TOOTHPICK AND CANTEEN OF "GREPTZ" COLA.

I SAW MR. KNIPL AND DOCTOR TARMOOTI AT THE HEAD OF TRAIL #7 JUST AFTER LUNCH.

IT'S NOT LIKE THEM TO MISS A MEAL.

THE FATE OF MISSING GUESTS IS THE TOPIC OF AFTER-DINNER CONVERSATION.

THEY MUST'VE STOPPED SOMEWHERE FOR A PIZZA.

OR FALLEN OFF A PRECIPICE IN THE DARK.

HOPEFULLY UNCONSCIOUS BEFORE THE WILD ANIMALS ARE LURED BY THE SCENT OF FRESH BLOOD.

OR MAYBE THEY WENT TO A MOVIE.

AT NIGHT, A SUCKING NOISE DISTURBS THE LIGHTER SLEEPERS.

THE WIND TRYING TO DISLODGE SOMETHING CAUGHT IN THE ROCKS.

LOST IN THE DARK, SOMEWHERE NEAR THE SUMMIT OF MOUNT KYAN, MR. KNIPL TRIES TO CHEER THE DISCONSOLATE DOCTOR TARMOOTI.

WE'RE LOST ...LOST...

PLEASE, THESE DAYS YOU CAN'T STRAY VERY FAR FROM CIVILIZATION. RIGHT HERE... I CAN ALREADY FEEL THE BEGINNING OF A CURB AND SIDEWALK.

YOU SEE, A PIZZA PLACE— STILL OPEN.

BE CAREFUL! THEY CALL IT PIZZA, BUT IT'S ACTUALLY A LOCAL CONCOCTION. AND WHAT'S THIS BRAND OF SODA: "GOLLY FLATUS"? I'VE NEVER HEARD OF IT, HAVE YOU? I BEG OF YOU, STICK TO A CHEESE SANDWICH OR ELSE GO HUNGRY... LISTEN TO ME, I'M A DOCTOR!

WHAT CAN I GET YOU?

MY GOOD MAN, LET ME EXPLAIN... WE COME FROM A DISTANT HOTEL ON THE OTHER SIDE OF THIS MOUNTAIN. OUT HIKING, FOOLISHLY LATE, WE LOST OUR WAY IN THE DARK. OUR TOOTHPICKS SOON BECAME SPLAYED AND HERE WE ARE, AT YOUR MERCY.

SO WHAT'LL YOU HAVE?

IT'S USELESS. HE DOES NOT UNDERSTAND. WE SPEAK TWO DIFFERENT LANGUAGES WHICH HAPPEN TO SHARE MANY OF THE SAME WORDS.

ACROSS THE STREET IS A BABYLONIAN RESTAURANT— BUT THEY ONLY DO TAKE-OUT.

YOU SEE, WE ARE LOST... DOOMED TO STARVE IN THE MIDST OF PLENTY!

MY GOOD MAN, I HAVE A PROPOSITION TO MAKE: YOU SELL US TWO PLAIN CHEESE SANDWICHES, THROW IN A FEW STURDY TOOTHPICKS AND WE'LL BE ON OUR WAY... PEACEFULLY. WHAT DO YOU SAY? IS IT A DEAL?

THAT'LL BE $5.10. WE HAVE NO TOOTHPICKS, SORRY.

FIVE MINUTES DOWN THE ROAD, THEY FIND A MOTEL WITH VACANCIES.

I MANAGED TO UNRAVEL A THREAD FROM THE HEM OF THIS POLYESTER SHEET TO USE AS DENTAL FLOSS.

THIS SHOWER'S A DEATH TRAP— THE MIXING VALVE IS ON BACKWARDS.

IN THE MORNING, A SEARCH PARTY, HAVING RETRACED THEIR STEPS, FINDS MR. KNIPL AND THE DOCTOR LANGUISHING AT A BREAKFAST BUFFET.

I HAD SOME SCRAMBLED EGGS FROM THE STEAM-TABLE... I WAS DESPERATE.

HERE, FRESH TOOTHPICKS— ALL YOU WANT— BUT TAKE IT EASY, TAKE IT EASY.

EMMANUEL CHIRRUP, THE SKID-PROOF-SLIPPER TYCOON, LIVES IN A MODEST SIX-STORY APARTMENT HOUSE ON AZURE AVENUE.

DON'T FORGET, YOU HAVE A 3:30 APPOINTMENT.

ONE GROUND-FLOOR REAR APARTMENT CONTAINS A MUSEUM-QUALITY REPRODUCTION OF THE SQUALID LIVING CONDITIONS OF HIS PARENTS AT THE TIME OF HIS BIRTH.

EVERY DETAIL, DOWN TO THE SMELL OF REHEATED POT ROAST AND "NOXZUMA" FACIAL CREAM!

A SMALL STUDIO ON THE SECOND FLOOR IS A REPLICA OF HIS FIRST 1950S-STYLE BACHELOR PAD.

THE OTHER FIVE APARTMENTS ON THIS FLOOR ARE MEMORIALS TO MY EARLY GIRLFRIENDS AND THEIR PARENTS' LOUSY TASTE.

A ONE-BEDROOM APARTMENT ON THE THIRD FLOOR IS RENTED TO HIS FIRST WIFE.

I'VE DONATED THE REST OF THIS FLOOR TO THE CITY DEPARTMENT OF CORRECTION FOR USE AS A HALF-WAY HOUSE.

THE FOURTH-FLOOR APARTMENTS ARE FILLED WITH THE REMAINS OF HIS VARIOUS PASSING FANCIES.

...A CHEESE-CAKE-SCULPTURE STUDIO, A CAMPAIGN HEADQUARTERS FOR THE SPLIT-PANTS PARTY, A VENETIAN-BLIND-RESTRINGING WORKSHOP, AND IN THIS APARTMENT, I ONCE BRED PEDIGREED COCKROACHES.

ON THE FIFTH FLOOR LIVES HIS SECOND WIFE, A CHINESE CHEF, A DESTITUTE TV WEATHERMAN OF THE 1960s, A UNION WINDOW-WASHER AND HIS HIGH SCHOOL FRENCH TEACHER.

ALL RENT-FREE! I STILL HAVE A CRUSH ON MADAME FLEISCH.

THE SIXTH-FLOOR APARTMENTS ARE ALL KEPT PERMANENTLY VACANT.

IT'S MY LATEST HOBBY. I RUN ADS IN THE SUNDAY NEWSPAPERS...

AND ENJOY SHOWING THESE EMPTY ROOMS TO TOTAL STRANGERS.

THE BEIGE RUG WOULD LOOK GOOD HERE.

LOOK, IF THIS MERINGUE-HANDLING JOB DOESN'T PAN OUT YOU CAN ALWAYS GET WORK AS A DRIVER.

A POORLY PAID MAN SPENDS HIS MORNINGS APPLYING HEART-SHAPED, ADHESIVE-BACKED STICKERS TO STRATEGICALLY CHOSEN SURFACES AROUND THE CITY.

THE SIDES OF ELECTRIC HAND-DRYERS, ABOVE BROKEN PAY-PHONES, ON THE MIRRORED WALLS OF HOT-DOG STANDS...

A CALL TO THIS NUMBER RINGS A SET OF BELLS IN THE TOWER OF THE NELUMBO BUILDING.

AN OCCUPIED CAB MEANDERS IDLY THROUGH THE BUSY MIDTOWN STREETS.

JUST BECAUSE I MANAGE A SMALL FLEET OF TAXIS DOESN'T MEAN THAT I'M IMMUNE TO THE APHRODISIAC EFFECT OF A CAB'S BACK SEAT.

PLEASE, DON'T SLOW DOWN! KEEP GOING... ANYWHERE!

AT THE FAMILIAR SOUND OF TOLLING BELLS, THE MANAGER TEARS HIMSELF FROM THE EMBRACE.

THAT'S FOR ME! ANOTHER PROSPECTIVE DRIVER CALLING.

WHAT'S WRONG WITH THIS DRIVER?

BONG BONG

HA, HA, HA... NOTHING... BUT IN TIME, HE WILL GROW TIRED OF MINDING HIS OWN BUSINESS; HE WILL MISS THE FRIENDLY SMALL TALK OF REGULAR CUSTOMERS; AND THEN, ONE DAY, HE'LL REFUSE TO DRIVE ANY FURTHER WITH-OUT A CLEAR-CUT DESTI-NATION IN MIND.

BONG BONG BONG

HE LEAVES THE CAB AND RETURNS TO HIS OFFICE BY MEANS OF PUBLIC TRANSPORTATION.

HOLD ON, I'M COMING!

BONG BONG BONG

INEVITABLY, THE RINGING STOPS JUST AS HE GETS THERE.

HELLO, HELLO...? COULDN'T WAIT.

PEOPLE ON THEIR WAY HOME AFTER A NIGHT ON THE TOWN; COMPULSIVE MILK-BUYERS...

AND NIGHT-WORKERS JUST STARTING THEIR "DAY," DESPERATE FOR SOMETHING TO READ, MIGHT BUY A COPY.

MOST WILL LOOK THROUGH IT IN SEARCH OF ACTUAL NEWS—WORLD EVENTS, SPORTS SCORES, STOCK QUOTATIONS—

"VEGETABLE SOUP SHOWER MELTS IGLOO PALACE—THOUSANDS SET FREE"?!

REALIZE THEY'VE MADE A MISTAKE AND LEAVE IT BEHIND.

SOMEONE ELSE WILL PICK IT UP.

THIS PASS-ALONG MECHANISM ACCOUNTS FOR SEVENTY-FIVE PERCENT OF THE PAPER'S LOYAL READERSHIP.

"INCEST PARTY RESUMES AT SYNAGOGUE LAUNDROMAT."

IT IS A NEWSPAPER WHICH SPEAKS MOST DIRECTLY TO THAT PORTION OF THE POPULATION INCAPABLE OF BUYING OR READING A NEWSPAPER — THE SOUNDLY SLEEPING.

"MOSQUITO GIVES BIRTH TO SENTIENT SAFETY-PIN."

IN SPITE OF THIS TENUOUS FORM OF DISTRIBUTION AND WHOLLY INCAPACITATED AUDIENCE, "THE EVENING COMBINATOR" CONTINUES TO PUBLISH AND THRIVE AS THE SOLE DAILY CHRONICLE OF THE CITY'S DREAM-LIFE.

"PANTYLESS WOMAN FEARS FOR SOULS OF CANNED SARDINES."

LATE THAT NIGHT ON THE PLAYTZER AVENUE LINE.

HMM? "COWBOY LIFEGUARD BREAKS UP CHIHUAHUA LOVE NEST."

WAKE UP, BROTHER. WAKE UP.

"CHRISTOPHER COLUMBUS DISCOVERS NUDIST COLONY IN DEPARTMENT STORE BASEMENT."

IT'S NOT TOO LATE. DON'T MISS YOUR STOP IN THIS LIFE.

YOU SEEM TO BE AN INTELLIGENT MAN, AND YET I SEE YOU READ "THE EVENING COMBINATOR."

I JUST NOW PICKED IT UP OFF THE FLOOR— SOMETHING TO READ— I HAVE A LONG TRIP.

YOU SEE THAT MAN OVER THERE WITH HIS PAJAMAS STICKING OUT FROM UNDER HIS TROUSERS? HE'S ONE OF THOSE UNFORTUNATE SOULS WHO'VE BEEN LED TO BELIEVE THAT THEIR OWN HOMES ARE NO LONGER CONDUCIVE TO PROPER SLEEP— A PAJAMA COMMUTER.

I'VE HEARD ABOUT THEM.

THEY'RE FORCED TO TRAVEL AT THIS UNGODLY HOUR, AND AT GREAT EXPENSE, TO HOTEL ROOMS OR SECOND APARTMENTS JUST TO GET A GOOD NIGHT'S SLEEP. CAN YOU IMAGINE?

I DIDN'T REALIZE.

AS I SEE IT, THEIR WHOLE LIFE IS ONE LONG FITFUL SLEEP.

WHAT DOES HE HAVE IN THAT SHOPPING BAG? AN AUTOMATIC JUICER? AN ELECTRIC CARD SHUFFLER? ...A BOMB?

OWOSSO MEAT MARKET

AND HERE YOU ARE— AN INTELLIGENT MAN LULLING HIMSELF INTO A STUPOR BY READING THESE LURID, SECOND-HAND ACCOUNTS OF THE HALF-BAKED WET-DREAMS OF THE SEX-STARVED MIDDLE CLASS!

PLEASE

WAKE UP! IT'S NOT TOO LATE. DON'T MISS YOUR STOP!

THE WAKE-UP CALL

I HAVE A BEAUTIFUL APARTMENT IN A QUIET NEIGHBORHOOD AND YET, EVERY NIGHT, I END UP SLEEPING IN MY OFFICE. I HAVEN'T BEEN HOME ONCE IN THE PAST SIX WEEKS. I JUST PAY THE RENT, THE ELECTRIC, THE TELEPHONE...

YOU'RE NOT THE ONLY ONE TONIGHT.

I KNOW FOR A FACT THAT GOURFIL, THE SLICING MACHINE MAN ON THE FOURTH FLOOR, SLEEPS THERE EVERY NIGHT. HE HAS A WIFE AND DAUGHTER IN LILAC MANOR WHO DON'T CARE; THEY'VE MADE AN ARRANGEMENT. THEN THERE'S MR. LUCKSHUN ON THE SEVENTH FLOOR...

DON'T MIND THE POCKET-BOOKS, MAKE YOURSELF AT HOME.

A WELL-DRESSED MAN FRANTICALLY PICKS THE TINY WHITE LETTERS OF HIS NAME FROM THE LOBBY DIRECTORY.

I HAD COMPLETELY FORGOTTEN ABOUT THIS BLATANT SIGN POINTING DIRECTLY TO MY OFFICE.

IT'S A BUSY NIGHT.

IF HE WANTS TO FIND ME, LET HIM LOOK ON ALL SIXTEEN FLOORS. WHY MAKE IT EASY FOR HIM?

I MAY HAVE AN UNWANTED CUSTOMER TONIGHT. SHOW HIM THE DIRECTORY. TELL HIM THE BUILDING IS OFFICIALLY CLOSED, TO COME BACK IN THE MORNING OR NEXT YEAR. DO YOU UNDERSTAND?

SURE, IT'S NO PROBLEM.

I BELIEVE HE'S A RELIABLE MAN. YOU WORK LATE TOO?

YES. JULIUS KNIPL, REAL ESTATE PHOTOGRAPHER ON EIGHT.

VICTOR RUBICON, I'M A SEVENTH FLOOR. I'M A BRASSIERE-STRAP ADJUSTER—HAS NOTHING TO DO WITH THE GARMENT BUSINESS OR WOMEN'S UNDERWEAR—ABSOLUTELY NOTHING! I'M A STATISTICIAN AGAINST WHOM THE ODDS HAVE TURNED.

MY DAY IS A SERIES OF EXTENDED COFFEE BREAKS. I SPEND HOURS IN THE STREET LOOKING FOR SIGNS OF DISCOMFORT, SLIPPAGE AND MALADJUSTMENT.

SO THIS IS THE SEVENTH FLOOR?

THE CORRELATION BETWEEN THE PHYSICAL DISCOMFORT CAUSED BY BRASSIERE STRAPS AND RETAIL SALES WAS DISCOVERED IN PARIS IN THE YEAR 1932 BY HYMAN SARI. EVERYTHING WE DO TODAY IS BASED UPON HIS GROUNDBREAKING WORK — WE JUST FOLLOW THE ESTABLISHED RULES. ANY SO-CALLED "GIRL-WATCHER" CAN NOW DO WHAT HE DID, BUT AT THE TIME, IT WAS A PROFOUNDLY ORIGINAL FEAT OF OBSERVATION.

2:15 P.M., PARTIAL RIGHT SHOULDER GLISSADE WITH MID-ARM RECOVERY.

I'VE LEARNED TO ANTICIPATE THE MOMENT OF DISCOMFORT, TO NOTE THE DEGREE OF SLIPPAGE AND RECORD THE FLEETING GESTURE WITH WHICH AN ADJUSTMENT IS MADE. IF YOU BLINK AT THE WRONG INSTANT, YOU'VE MISSED EVERYTHING. IF YOU GET TOO CLOSE, YOU CHASE THE WOMAN AWAY.

4:27 P.M., DISPLACED LACE BITE, REPLANTED ONE-QUARTER INCH TO THE LEFT.

I COMPILE THESE FINDINGS AND SELL THEM TO TRADE GROUPS, RETAILERS AND MANUFACTURERS: "THE ASSOCIATION OF CARDBOARD SHOE MANUFACTURERS," "ZALIVA GUMMED TAPE CO.," "WOMB'S JUVENILE CLOTHING STORE"...

"MAHOT'S ARTIFICIAL FLOWER GARDEN."

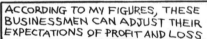

ACCORDING TO MY FIGURES, THESE BUSINESSMEN CAN ADJUST THEIR EXPECTATIONS OF PROFIT AND LOSS.

16% INCREASE IN SLIPPAGE CITY-WIDE...

BAD SEASONS CAN'T BE AVOIDED, BUT THE SHOCK CAN BE TEMPERED.

SALES DOWN 20%.

AND SO, YOU ASK, WHAT AM I DOING HERE AT THIS HOUR? WHY AREN'T I AT HOME IN BED WITH MY WIFE?

"KING SOLOMON'S KITCHENWARE."

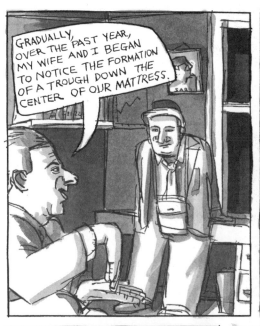

GRADUALLY, OVER THE PAST YEAR, MY WIFE AND I BEGAN TO NOTICE THE FORMATION OF A TROUGH DOWN THE CENTER OF OUR MATTRESS.

SHE WAS THE ONE WHO SUGGESTED THAT IT WAS TIME TO HAVE IT REPLACED.

FIFTEEN YEARS OF TURNING AND ROTATION— FOR WHAT?

FORTUNATELY, WE FOUND OURSELVES IN A SEASON OF SPECIAL SALES AND MANUFACTURER'S GOOD WILL.

FLUXION SLEEP CENTER

2 for 1 Free box spring

guaranteed PNEUM STYLE Fine bedding

BEFORE A DOZEN SALESMEN, IN A DOZEN DIFFERENT SHOWROOMS, WE ASSUMED OUR FAMILIAR POSITIONS OF SLEEP IN AN ATTEMPT TO NARROW OUR CHOICES.

I'LL LEAVE YOU TWO ALONE.

I CAME TO SUSPECT THAT ALL MATTRESSES ORIGINATED IN A SINGLE FACTORY LOCATED ON THE WINDSWEPT SHORE OF A VAST INLAND SEA AND DIFFERED ONLY IN THEIR LABEL.

TICKING CO

EACH MANUFACTURER WOULD OFFER THE IDENTICAL MATTRESS UNDER A VARIETY OF DIFFERENT NAMES, DEPENDING ON WHICH STORE YOU HAPPENED TO BE IN, IT WOULD BE CALLED A "SANDMAN'S PALLET," AN "AESTHETIC SLEEPER," AN "EASY TURNER" OR A "JUMBO LYRE."

THAT'S THE SAME AS OUR "SPRING VALET."

OUR ENTHUSIASM OVER THE ORTHOPEDIC QUALITIES OF EACH MATTRESS PALLED BEFORE THE SALESMAN'S CHEERY PITCH.

REMEMBER, YOU SPEND HALF YOUR LIFE IN BED.

WE SETTLED ON AN EXTRA-FIRM "MORTAL COIL" AND BOX SPRING TO BE DELIVERED IN TWO DAYS.

BOOM

A CELEBRATORY CHEER RISES FROM THE ASSEMBLED CROWD AT ORMOND BELL'S "STAY-AWAKE-ATORIUM."

HOORAY!

YES, BROTHERS AND SISTERS, IT HAS COME TO THIS. REASON WILL NOT WORK, FOR YOU CAN NOT REASON WITH A SLEEPING BEAST.

ONLY ON RARE OCCASIONS CAN WE DEPEND UPON LIFE TO STARTLE US INTO COMPLETE WAKEFULNESS: THE NEWS OF A DEATH, THE DIAGNOSIS OF A FATAL DISEASE, OR, BOO!, A SIMPLE FRIGHT. THE REST OF THE TIME, WE'RE LEFT TO SINK INTO THE SLUMBER OF ROUTINE DAY-TO-DAY EXISTENCE.

TONIGHT, BROTHER HARTIK HAS DONE HIS PART TO AWAKEN THE TWENTY THOUSAND SOULS WHO RESIDE IN THE VICINITY OF VACUUNA AND DOLLY STREETS—A GRAVE AND SERIOUS MISSION. YOU SEE, THE DESTRUCTION OF LIFE AND PROPERTY IS AN UNFORTUNATE SIDE-EFFECT OF THESE HIGH-DECIBEL NOISEMAKERS.

THE PERMANENTLY OPEN WINDOW.

BUT WE SAY, "THE FOURTH OF JULY," MUST BE EVERY DAY. LET'S ROUSE EACH MAN, WOMAN AND CHILD FROM THEIR BED—AND THEN ROUSE THEM AGAIN TO THE REAL LIGHT OF DAY! IT'S NOT EASY TO PRY OPEN THAT STUBBORN SECOND, INNER EYELID—THE ONE THAT PREVENTS MAN FROM SEEING WHAT'S RIGHT IN FRONT OF HIM!

THE DREAMER ACCEPTS THE REALITY BEFORE HIS EYES AS BEING IMMUTABLE. A GOLD-FISH HAS BEEN ELECTED PRESIDENT OF THE UNITED STATES. "WHY NOT," THE DREAMER SAYS, "MAKES PERFECT SENSE."

BUT WHEN THIS NOCTURNAL THINKING CARRIES OVER INTO "WAKING LIFE," THE RESULTS ARE DISASTROUS—A POPULATION OF SLEEP-WALKERS WHO ACCEPT EVERYTHING—FROM THE WORKINGS OF THE ECONOMIC SYSTEM TO THE COLOR OF A DOLLAR BILL.

HELP YOURSELF NO LIMIT

IT IS OUR MODEST GOAL TO PROVIDE EACH MAN, WOMAN AND CHILD IN THIS CITY WITH ONE MOMENT OF COMPLETE WAKEFULNESS EACH DAY—A BREAK IN THEIR HABITUAL SEMI-SLUMBER. WE ARE NOT AGAINST SLEEP, IN FACT, THEY'LL SLEEP BETTER FOR IT.

LEAVE THAT WINDOW OPEN! I DON'T CARE HOW COLD IT IS OUTSIDE!

ABOVE A LONG-VACANT SUPERMARKET, AT THE CORNER OF HALOOSE AND VYNUT STREETS,

IN THE OFFICES OF "THE EVENING COMBINATOR,"

THE ECONOMICS OF SLEEP, PART TWO: COUNTING POCKET-CHANGE WITH CLOSED EYES...

DR. PHAROS, THE EDITOR-IN-CHIEF, IS AWAKENED FROM HIS WORK BY THE SOUND OF A DISTANT EXPLOSION.

BOOM

IN THE STREET, A TRUCKLOAD OF DISCARDED MATTRESSES IS QUIETLY UNLOADED.

WE WORK HAND-IN-HAND WITH THE SHOWROOMS. THE MINUTE THEY MAKE A SALE, WORD IS SENT HERE.

LOUIS BRICANT, HIGH-SCHOOL MATH TEACHER: GOES TO SLEEP EARLY, NO HISTORY OF SHEET TUGGING. BY MUTUAL CONSENT HAS ALWAYS TAKEN LEFT SIDE OF BED. WIFE'S A LIGHT SLEEPER.

THE DELIVERY AND REMOVAL IS PERFORMED BY A GROUP OF PROFESSIONAL "DREAM BOYS" OR "FREE ASSOCIATORS"—MALE PROSTITUTES WE HIRE TO MAKE INITIAL CONTACT WITH THE SUBJECT.

STILL WARM.

THE MATTRESSES ARE FILED BY NAME AND DATE OF USE.

IT'S A CONVENIENT WAY TO KEEP TRACK OF LEADS. SHEETS AND PILLOWCASES ARE HARDER TO COME BY AND ARE RUINED IN THE WASH; THE SLEEP RESIDUE IS THROWN OUT WITH THE DIRTY WATER.

DR. PHAROS UPBRAIDS A ROOKIE REPORTER.

WHO CARES HOW HE SPENDS HIS DAY? AN ANALYSIS OF THE MATTRESS SHOWS A MAELSTROM OF ELECTRICAL BRAIN ACTIVITY—A PROLIFIC DREAMER! OUR READERS ARE NOT ASKING FOR A PSYCHOANALYSIS—JUST THE FACTS.

RECESSED GLOWWORM-LAMPS FLUORESCE LATE INTO THE NIGHT AT THE OFFICES OF SELLADORE & ASSOCIATES.

AH, THE SWEET SOUND OF DEMOLITION, MAKING ROOM FOR THE NEW, IMPROVED CITY.

THIS FAX WILL COME AS A TERRIBLE BLOW TO THE POOR MAN. IT'S THE OLD STORY: A WELL-RESPECTED ARCHITECT AND URBAN PLANNER WORKING FOR THIRTY YEARS, A LEADER IN HIS FIELD WHO'S MANAGED TO HAVE ALMOST NOTHING BUILT—NOTHING CONCRETE TO SHOW.

HIS WORK IS OF A MORE VISIONARY NATURE. YOU KNOW, BANK BUILDINGS WITHOUT DOORS, GOVERNMENT OFFICES IN THE FORM OF BEACH CABANAS, THAT SORT OF THING, ALL ON PAPER.

ONLY NOW, FOR THE FIRST TIME IN HIS CAREER, HE'S GOTTEN A PROJECT OFF THE GROUND. PERHAPS YOU'VE SEEN THE LARGE HOLE ON THE CORNER OF HALOOSE AND VYNUT STREETS? THAT'S HIS. A LARGE MIXED-USE DEVELOPMENT CALLED "CARFARE CITY."— A MULTI-BILLION-DOLLAR PROJECT.

ON THIS SITE CARFARE CITY OPENING 2010

AND THEN THE STORIES BEGAN TO APPEAR IN "THE EVENING COMBINATOR." SELLADORE LAUGHS THEM OFF. "I SHOULD HAVE SUCH DREAMS. HOW MANY WOMEN DID THEY SAY WERE INVOLVED? AND MEN, TOO?" HE JOKES.

"THE SUBTERRANEAN RESTAURANT WAS FILLED WITH THE SOUND OF NYLON RUBBING AGAINST NYLON— FORTY WOMEN DINERS CROSSING THEIR LEGS. MR. SELLADORE WAS ALREADY ON HIS HANDS AND KNEES MAKING THE ROUNDS."

BUT THE INVESTORS ARE GETTING COLD FEET. MAYBE IT'S ALL AN EXCUSE TO STEP IN AND REVISE THE MORE VISIONARY ASPECTS OF HIS PLAN. IT TROUBLES THEM TO SEE THE NAME OF THEIR ARCHITECT IN THE PAPER, EACH NIGHT LINKED TO SUCH SALACIOUS ACTIVITY.

BUT IT'S ONLY A DREAM— NOT EVEN MY DREAM.

ALL THE MORE REASON TO WORRY.

CITIZEN'S GROUPS HAVE CALLED THE MORAL BASIS OF HIS PLAN INTO QUESTION.

IS THIS WHAT WILL TRANSPIRE ON THE STREETS OF "CAR-FARE CITY"? IS THIS SELLADORE'S NEW, IDEALISTIC FORM OF URBAN LIFE?

AND SO HERE IT IS: AN ORDER TO POSTPONE TOMORROW'S FOUNDATION POURING. THEY NEED TIME TO REASSESS THE PLAN FROM AN ETHICAL POINT OF VIEW.

FIFTY PAGES OF ALTERATIONS: MORE STREET LIGHTS, FEWER ALLEYWAYS, PEDESTRIAN CURFEWS...

IN A PROJECT OF THIS MAGNITUDE THERE'S ALWAYS ROOM FOR COMPROMISE.

RAP RAP

THE ARCHITECT, SELLADORE, ADDRESSES THE FOUR WALLS OF HIS STUDIO.

INTERMISSION'S OVER! IT'S TIME FOR THE CURTAIN TO RISE ON A NEW ACT OF HUMAN LIFE. AND THIS TIME, JUST FOR FUN, LET'S TRY PUTTING THE "BUS STOP" PROPS IN THE "VESTIBULE" AND VICE VERSA.

THE CHILD PLAYING IN THE PARK CRIES WHEN IT'S TIME TO "GO HOME." THE DISEASE OF HOMESICKNESS CAN NOT BE CURED WITH A PLANE TICKET. IT IS NOW IN OUR POWER TO ESCAPE WHAT FOR HUNDREDS OF YEARS WAS CONSIDERED THE INEVITABLE.

HE'S IN THERE. I CAN HEAR HIM.

RAP RAP

MODERN MAN NO LONGER HAS TO GO "HOME." HE CAN LIVE IN A CONDITION OF TRANSPORTATIONAL FLUX, TRAVELING BETWEEN "HOME" AND THE "WORLD" BUT NEVER HAVING TO REACH EITHER END POINT. MY "CARFARE CITY" IS A FORETASTE OF THIS NEW LIFE.

INSPIRED BY THE ONCE-DESPISED ENVIRONMENT WHICH DEVELOPS NATURALLY BENEATH ELEVATED SUBWAY LINES, I'VE DEVISED A NEW FORM OF URBAN DWELLING. 5,000 FAMILIES AND AN EQUAL NUMBER OF BUSINESSES COMPRESSED INTO A SIX-BLOCK AREA — ALL INTER-CONNECTED BY AN ELECTRIC STREET-CAR SYSTEM AND GROVES OF APPLE TREES.

THE RESIDENT ENTERS "CARFARE CITY" BY MEANS OF A "GRAND TERMINAL" MODELED AFTER THE EXHILARATING SPACE OF A LATE-19th-CENTURY TRAIN STATION. DAILY LIFE IN THIS "CITY" TAKES ON THE PLEASURE OF A PROSPECTIVE JOURNEY. YOUR RENT IS PAID BY PURCHASING A SYMBOLIC TICKET — ROUND-TRIP, ONE-WAY OR OPEN EXCURSION.

THESE COMFORTABLE CARS WILL ONLY RUN AT FIFTEEN-MINUTE INTERVALS TO ENCOURAGE THE CONTEMPLATIVE PLEASURES OF IDLE WAITING. ONCE ON, ALL SEATS ARE WINDOW SEATS.

NEXT CAR IN 13 MINUTES

THE ELECTRIC STREET-CAR SYSTEM PASSES THROUGH EACH LIVING AND BUSINESS SPACE. EACH APARTMENT WILL BE THOUGHT OF AS A "STATION" OR "STOP," FAMILIAR IN VARYING DEGREES TO ALL PASSING BY.

IN THIS WAY, THE LIVING CONDITIONS OF EACH RESIDENT CAN BE SEEN BY ANYONE WHO CARES TO LOOK. THE MYSTERIES OF PRIVATE LIFE BECOME THE DETAILS OF A PASSING LANDSCAPE.

PEOPLE ASK, "HOW CAN ANYONE LIVE WITH A STREETCAR LINE RUNNING THROUGH THEIR BEDROOM? WHAT BECOMES OF PRIVACY? HOW CAN ONE TOLERATE THE NOISE?"

I ANSWER, "SMALL DRESSING AND BATHROOMS WILL BE PROVIDED, BUT OTHER THAN THAT, THE PUBLIC AND PRIVATE ASPECTS OF LIFE WILL BECOME INTERTWINED ACCORDING TO A SCHEDULE OF PASSING STREET-CARS."

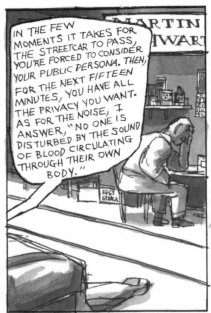

IN THE FEW MOMENTS IT TAKES FOR THE STREETCAR TO PASS, YOU'RE FORCED TO CONSIDER YOUR PUBLIC PERSONA. THEN, FOR THE NEXT FIFTEEN MINUTES, YOU HAVE ALL THE PRIVACY YOU WANT. AS FOR THE NOISE, I ANSWER, "NO ONE IS DISTURBED BY THE SOUND OF BLOOD CIRCULATING THROUGH THEIR OWN BODY."

BETWEEN EVERY FIFTH "STATION," THERE IS A CHASM SPANNED BY AN ELEVATED RAIL-LINE, BELOW WHICH LIES A BUSINESS STREET DIS-SOLVED IN THE VARIEGATED HALF-LIGHT CAST BY THE STRUCTURE ABOVE.

BY MEANS OF A COMPLEX BRAIDING OF "STATION" PLATFORMS AND ELEVATED RAILWAYS, THE WEATHER IS ALLOWED TO REACH THE SURFACE OF EACH BUSINESS STREET.

THE STRUCTURE'S EXTERIOR IS A VERTICAL CITY PARK: APPLE TREES, WATERFALLS AND WINDING PATHS. AFTER AN EVENING OF HAPPILY SHUTTLING BETWEEN THE PERFUMED BOUDOIR OF MRS. VERA USKY, THE TAKE-OUT COUNTER OF THE JUVELLY DONUT SHOP, NINK'S ATHENAEUM . . .

AND THE GUANO HANDBALL COURTS, YOU SUDDENLY ARRIVE, BY CHANCE, AT YOUR OWN STOP. FOR A MOMENT, YOU FAIL TO RECOGNIZE YOUR OWN FURNITURE AND POSSESSIONS. FOR A MOMENT, YOU'RE HAPPY TO BE IN THIS STRANGELY FAMILIAR PLACE WITH ITS ENAMEL SIGN BEARING YOUR NAME IN TWO-FOOT-HIGH LETTERS.

WHO'S THERE?

RAP RAP

OBLIVIOUS TO THE SOUND OF THE EXPLOSION, VICTOR RUBICON CONTINUES HIS SAD STORY.

THAT FIRST NIGHT, I KNEW THAT SOMETHING WAS NOT RIGHT WITH THE MATTRESS. THROUGH THE SHEET I COULD FEEL AN ODDLY PLACED VENTILATION HOLE JUST BELOW MY PILLOW.

WHAT THE HELL WAS THAT?

I NEVER READ "THE EVENING COMBINATOR." I KNOW WHAT IT'S ABOUT AND I'M NOT INTERESTED. I HAVE ENOUGH TROUBLE KEEPING UP WITH THE NEWS OF THIS WORLD.

SAME HERE, I FOUND THIS ON THE SUBWAY.

BUT SPENDING AS MUCH TIME AS I DO ON THE STREET, I'LL INEVITABLY SEE A HEADLINE OR COME ACROSS A WEEK-OLD COPY TUCKED INTO SOME COFFEE SHOP BOOTH.

THE EVENING COMBINATOR
ONE MILLION SARDINE SOULS SAVED IN CAN OPENER BAN.

AND SO IT CAME AS A TERRIBLE SHOCK TO SEE MY NAME IN A FRONT-PAGE STORY. THAT WAS TUESDAY— THE DAY AFTER THE NEW MATTRESS CAME.

"BRASSIERE STRAP ADJUSTER, VICTOR RUBICON, STAGES LOVE-PLAY IN HOTEL LOBBY."

YOU SEE, I RARELY REMEMBER MY DREAMS, BUT HERE THEY WERE—RECOUNTED IN TERRIFYING DETAIL —AND SAD TO SAY, ALL TRUE!

"THE TABLEAU WAS FRAMED BY SIX BELLHOPS DRESSED IN NOTHING MORE THAN THEIR GLOVES. A PROCESSION OF STRANGE WOMEN PASSED THROUGH THE GANTLET OF RUBICON'S PASSION, CRYING FOR MERCY, YET TAKING THEIR TIME."

EACH EVENING, JUST BEFORE DINNER, I WOULD LEAVE THE HOUSE UNDER SOME FALSE PRETENSE

WE'RE SHORT ON MILK.

RUSH TO A CORNER STORE AND BUY THE LATEST COPY.

"VIC RUBICON UNDERGOES CIRCUMCISION AT HANDS OF WELL-KNOWN MOVIE STARLET."

A STYLISHLY DRESSED, SIXTY-YEAR-OLD MAN BEGAN TO APPEAR IN MY DREAMS EACH NIGHT. A STEP-FATHER FIGURE; A FORE-GOTTEN COLLEGE PROFESSOR TRANSMOGRIFIED INTO A RUTHLESS CASANOVA; A MAN SEEN ON THE BUS TWENTY YEARS AGO, WHO KNOWS?

I THOUGHT THEY MADE THESE STORIES UP.

THE MAN'S NAME IS SELLADORE—THAT'S HOW I DREAM IT, ONE NAME. HOW I FIRST CAME TO DREAM OF HIM IS A MYSTERY. I'D NEVER EVEN HEARD THE NAME, AND YET, NIGHT AFTER NIGHT, THERE HE WAS.

SELLADORE AS AN EXHIBITIONIST NIGHT-CLUB SINGER; THE SEXUAL EXPLOITS OF SELLADORE; SELLADORE AS AN ANTI-SOCIAL HEDONIST...

DON'T FORGET THE MOP.

GOAT CURRY AND A FEMALE LIBRARIAN— THAT'S WHAT I'M IN THE MOOD FOR.

EACH NIGHT, I'M JUST A HANGER-ON, AN ENVIOUS FLUNKY, PART OF AN ENTOURAGE OF PLEASURE SEEKERS OUT ON THE TOWN. OF COURSE IT WAS HUMILIATING TO SEE THEM IN PRINT, BUT WE ALL HAVE THESE LICENTIOUS DREAMS.

THEY'RE WITH ME.

THE JANITOR OF THIS BUILDING HAD SEEN IT ALL BEFORE.

RELAX, YOU DON'T HAVE TO THROW THE MATTRESS OUT. JUST SPEND A NIGHT AWAY FROM HOME—IN A NICE HOTEL OR AT A FRIEND'S HOUSE. GIVE IT A CHANCE TO AIR OUT AND EVERYTHING'LL BE OKAY.

TWO DAYS LATER, I GET A PHONE CALL. STATISTICALLY, IT WAS A ONE-IN-A-MILLION CHANCE. A PROMINENT ARCHITECT, WHO GOES BY THE NAME "SELLADORE," HAPPENS TO HAVE SEEN THE ARTICLES—TELLS ME EVERYONE'S SEEN THEM. HE'S AMUSED, BUT NO ONE ELSE IS. OF COURSE, HE DOESN'T HOLD ME RESPONSIBLE BUT IS CURIOUS TO KNOW WHAT SUBCONSCIOUS GRUDGE I HAVE AGAINST HIM.

I APOLOGIZE. I'VE NEVER HEARD OF YOU OR YOUR WORK. THE ACCOUNTS YOU'VE READ OF MY DREAMS ARE ALL TRUE AND ACCURATE, BUT FOR ANYONE TO IDENTIFY YOU WITH THE "SELLADORE" OF MY DREAMS IS A TERRIBLE MISTAKE. IT'S JUST A NAME. THE UNCONSCIOUS MIND MAKES UP SUCH NAMES ALL THE TIME.

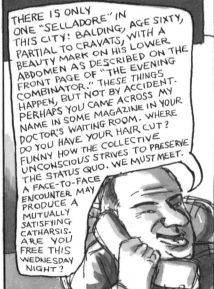

THERE IS ONLY ONE "SELLADORE" IN THIS CITY: BALDING, AGE SIXTY, PARTIAL TO CRAVATS, WITH A BEAUTY MARK ON HIS LOWER ABDOMEN AS DESCRIBED ON THE FRONT PAGE OF "THE EVENING COMBINATOR." THESE THINGS HAPPEN, BUT NOT BY ACCIDENT. PERHAPS YOU CAME ACROSS MY NAME IN SOME MAGAZINE IN YOUR DOCTOR'S WAITING ROOM. WHERE DO YOU HAVE YOUR HAIR CUT? FUNNY HOW THE COLLECTIVE UNCONSCIOUS STRIVES TO PRESERVE THE STATUS QUO. WE MUST MEET. A FACE-TO-FACE ENCOUNTER MAY PRODUCE A MUTUALLY SATISFYING CATHARSIS. ARE YOU FREE THIS WEDNESDAY NIGHT?

I TOLD HIM, "PLEASE DON'T BOTHER ME. YOUR ARGUMENT IS WITH THE PUBLISHERS OF 'THE EVENING COMBINATOR,' WHO TAKE IT UPON THEMSELVES TO MAKE THIS SORT OF INFORMATION PUBLIC." HE ASKED ME WHERE I BROUGHT MY DRY CLEANING AND I HUNG UP.

THIS IS WEDNESDAY NIGHT.

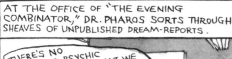

AT THE OFFICE OF "THE EVENING COMBINATOR," DR. PHAROS SORTS THROUGH SHEAVES OF UNPUBLISHED DREAM-REPORTS.

THERE'S NO OCCULT OR PSYCHIC HOCUS-POCUS TO WHAT WE DO. IF YOU ASKED A MAN ON THE STREET TO REPORT ON THE AFFAIRS OF CITY HALL, HE'D BE LOST—HAVE NO IDEA WHERE TO BEGIN. BUT FOR A REPORTER, IT'S ROUTINE WORK; HE'S CULTIVATED A HOST OF RELIABLE SOURCES.

MOST APARTMENT DWELLERS DON'T KNOW THAT THERE'S AN EXIT-DOOR TO EVERY BED-ROOM CLOSET; IT'S THERE, BEHIND THE COATS—SOMEONE HOLDS THE KEY.

AND WE DON'T HAVE ROOM TO PRINT HALF THE DREAMS YOU CAN OVERHEAR IN ANY COFFEE SHOP AT BREAKFAST TIME. PEOPLE TALK, WALK, WRITE AND TELEPHONE IN THEIR SLEEP. HOTEL MAIDS, NIGHT WATCHMEN, HOSPITAL ATTENDANTS, TV REPAIRMEN, UNETHICAL PSYCHIATRISTS ARE ALL VALUABLE INFORMANTS.

ALL NIGHT HE CRIED, "ARE THE ANTELOPE RIPE? ARE THEY IN SEASON YET?"

YOU LEARN TO READ THE SLEEP IN THE CORNER OF A RECENTLY AWOKEN EYE, THE PILLOW CREASES ON A STRANGER'S CHEEK, THE NUANCES OF A SNORE. THERE'S A BASIC VOCABULARY.

ANOTHER FINE INSTALLATION LUKSE WINDOW

MOST PEOPLE ARE INCAPABLE OF FAITHFULLY RECOUNTING THE NARRATIVE DETAILS OF THEIR OWN DREAMS, MUCH LESS THE FEEL AND TEXTURE OF THE EXPERIENCE; THEY LACK THE LITERARY SKILL. OUR REPORTERS ARE FAILED NOVELISTS, SOCIAL WORKERS WITH A FLAIR FOR CREATIVE WRITING AND PATHOLOGICAL STORYTELLERS—MEN WHO'VE LEARNED TO TAKE NOTES IN THE DARK.

THE FLUTTERING RED, WHITE AND BLUE PLASTIC PENNANTS OF THE GRAND-OPENING BANNER WHICH HUNG FROM THE FACADE OF HER DEAD FATHER'S TOOTHBRUSH REPAIR SHOP SET OFF A SERIES OF SYMPATHETIC VIBRATIONS IN THE NERVES OF HER LOWER SPINAL CORD.

WITH THE ARRIVAL OF A NEW MATTRESS, A REPORTER HAS A CHANCE TO GET HIS FOOT IN THE DOOR. HIS PRESENCE IS SOME-HOW LESS NOTICEABLE IN THOSE FIRST FEW DAYS.

WHAT'S THAT FUNNY SMELL?

SNIFF. MUST BE THE NEW MATTRESS.

PEOPLE LIKE TO BELIEVE THAT THESE INNERMOST THOUGHTS—WHICH ARE SOMETIMES INACCESSIBLE EVEN TO THEMSELVES—ARE PRIVATE, BUT IN FACT, IT'S ALL AN OPEN BOOK.

DON'T SHOW ME ANOTHER FLYING DREAM, PLEASE. ANYTHING NEW TONIGHT ON THE RUBICON STORY?

NO, HE NEVER WENT HOME—MUST BE OUT OF TOWN—BUT WE HAVE A JUICY LEAD ON A POCKETBOOK MANUFACTURER WHO DREAMT HE WAS A CALF.

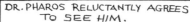
THE ARCHITECT, SELLADORE, ENTERS THE URINE-SPRAYED LOBBY OF "THE EVENING COMBINATOR."

THEY'RE UNAWARE OF THE REPERCUSSIONS OF WHAT THEY PRINT. I'LL LODGE A COMPLAINT AND DEMAND A RETRACTION.

DR. PHAROS RELUCTANTLY AGREES TO SEE HIM.

YOU CAN SEE I'M BUSY. WE HAVE DEADLINES, TOO, JUST LIKE A NORMAL NEWSPAPER.

ALL I'M ASKING IS THAT YOU MENTION, SOMEWHERE AT THE BEGINNING OF THE ARTICLE, THAT THIS IS, OF COURSE, JUST A DREAM ACCOUNT AND THAT NO ONE, INCLUDING THE DREAMER, IS RESPONSIBLE FOR ITS CONTENT. THINK OF ALL THE HEARTACHE AND HUMILIATION YOU'D AVOID.

DOES "THE DAILY PIGEON" PREFACE EACH ARTICLE IT PRINTS BY SAYING THAT ALL OF THE PARTICIPANTS HEREIN DESCRIBED WERE FULLY AWAKE? NO, IT'S UNDERSTOOD. THEY LEAVE IT TO THE READER TO FIGURE OUT. WE DO THE SAME.

I ADMIT THAT I'LL OCCASIONALLY READ YOUR PAPER. AS A PROFESSIONAL ARCHITECT, I'M CURIOUS TO HEAR OF THE GRANDIOSE DREAMS OF BUILDERS AND DEVELOPERS. MUCH OF OUR CITY'S SKYLINE IS A RESULT OF THOSE DREAMS.

IT ALSO HAPPENS, AS IN YOUR CASE, THAT A BUILDING IS NOT ERECTED BECAUSE OF SOMEONE'S DREAM.

BUT FOR THE MOST PART, YOU MAKE FRONT-PAGE NEWS OUT OF THE EFFLUVIA OF A SLEEPING MIND. YOUR PREDILECTION FOR SEX, SCANDAL AND VIOLENCE IS DISCOURAGING. WHAT IS THE POINT?

YOU MAY NOT CARE FOR THE SUBJECT MATTER, BUT IN OUR DREAMS WE ARE ALL POETS.

"ETHICAL INDIFFERENCE REIGNS SUPREME." "THE WILD BEAST WITHIN US GOES FORTH TO SATISFY HIS DESIRES." IS EVERYTHING YOU READ IN YOUR OTHER NEWSPAPERS ANALYZED AS TO ITS ULTIMATE MEANING, OR IS IT JUST A RECORD OF WHAT'S TRANSPIRED IN THE PAST 24 HOURS?

HERE'S A MARVELOUS STORY: A MAN WHO'S BEEN MURDERED FIFTY-SIX TIMES IN THE LAST WEEK! ONLY IN SLEEP CAN THE IMAGINATION REVEAL THESE TERRIBLE TRUTHS WHICH LIE HIDDEN BEYOND THE SCOPE OF REASON. WHO ELSE WILL GIVE VOICE TO THE DREAM-LIFE OF THE COMMON MAN?

BUT YOU'RE IN LUCK TONIGHT. MR. RUBICON DID NOT SLEEP AT HOME. WE HAVE NOTHING TO REPORT.

IS THERE ROOM FOR ANOTHER FALLING DREAM ON PAGE 17?

AT THE "STAY-AWAKE-ATORIUM," ORMOND BELL ENTERS HIS 285th CONSECUTIVE HOUR WITHOUT SLEEP.

CONSIDER THE DISAPPEARANCE OF FORMAL-WEAR IN THIS SOCIETY. ALL CLOTHING NOW, IN ONE WAY OR ANOTHER, APPROACHES THE STYLE OF THE PAJAMA—THE DRESS OF CERTAIN EASTERN POTENTATES WHO SPENT THEIR ENTIRE LIVES LOST IN A LUXURIOUS DREAM.

MOST OF US CAN'T AFFORD SUCH LUXURY. MOST OF US ARE LABORING UNDER THE DELUSION THAT WE ARE FULLY AWAKE. BUT OUR SO-CALLED "WAKING LIFE" IS NO MORE THAN A SLIGHT LIFTING OF THE VEIL.

WE RISE FROM OUR BED, BRUSH OUR TEETH, PUT ON OUR CLOTHES, HAVE BREAKFAST AND LEAVE FOR WORK. IT'S A WONDER MORE PEOPLE AREN'T STRUCK DEAD EACH MORNING BY AUTOMOBILES!

FOR, YOU SEE, THE HOURS WE SPEND AT WORK AND AT PLAY ARE SPENT IN A FORM OF SEMI-SLUMBER. THE LIFE WE SEE BEFORE US IS NO MORE REAL THAN A DREAM. "WHO WAS THAT UNCLE HARRY UPON WHOSE LAP I SAT AS A CHILD? WHERE DID HE GO?" A DREAM WITH VAGUE LINKS AND RECURRING IMAGERY, BUT A DREAM JUST THE SAME.

THIS GREAT AORISTIC GLOOM, BETWEEN COMPLETE WAKEFULNESS AND TRUE SLEEP, WE CALL THE "PRAEDORMIUM." IT IS A TWILIGHT WORLD OF LAPSED ATTENTION, DAY-DREAMS AND CAT-NAPS. SURE, NO ONE LIKES TO GET UP IN THE MORNING. I DON'T, I ADMIT IT! BUT IT'S TIME NOW! IT'S WAY PAST NOON IN THE HISTORY OF HUMANKIND. TIME TO GET UP—AND THIS TIME I MEAN FOR REAL!

THE PIECEMEAL AWAKENINGS WE'VE SPONSORED OVER THE PAST FEW WEEKS WERE FINE AND GOOD, BUT NOT ENOUGH. IT IS OUR PLAN TO ROUSE THE ENTIRE CITY AT ONCE BY MEANS OF A SERIES OF COORDINATED EXPLOSIONS.

TONIGHT, AS WE SPEAK, BROTHERS YOKIM AND KOHL ARE IN THE FIELD. THEY IN SEVEN MINUTES, WILL AWAKEN THE RESIDENTS OF HALOOSE AND VYNUT STREETS. WE FIND THERE A HOSIERY SHOP, A COLD-DRINK STAND, A CON-STRUCTION SITE AND A VACANT SUPERMARKET—AN INTERSECTION OF STRATEGIC IMPORTANCE IN OUR STRUGGLE.

TWO FRIGHTENED MEN DECIDE TO THROW A SHOPPING BAG FILLED WITH EXPLOSIVES OVER THE WOODEN HOARDING OF A CONSTRUCTION SITE.

LET'S GET OUTTA HERE—

ON THIS SITE
CARFARE CITY
OPENING 2010

The Evening Combinator   105

THE ARCHITECT, SELLADORE, ARRIVES AT "THE OILCLOTH BUILDING" ON ROSSEL AVENUE.

OF COURSE HE'S NOT HOME—WE HAD TENTATIVELY SCHEDULED A MEETING FOR TONIGHT, HERE, AT HIS OFFICE.

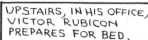
ON THE LOBBY FLOOR, HE NOTICES THE SCATTERED LETTERS OF A NAME.

"R-U-B-I-C-O-N... 7-0-1."

CAN I HELP YOU?

UPSTAIRS, IN HIS OFFICE, VICTOR RUBICON PREPARES FOR BED.

I BROUGHT SOME BLANKETS WITH ME. MY WIFE UNDERSTANDS.

THEY TURN THE HEAT OFF AT FIVE.

KNOCK KNOCK

GOOD EVENING, GENTLEMEN, MY NAME IS SELLADORE. MR. RUBICON, I PRESUME?

YES. YOU'RE SHORTER THAN I DREAMT.

AND ARE YOU ALSO A PRODUCT OF HIS LATE-NIGHT EATING AND SEXUAL FRUSTRATIONS?

NO, WE JUST MET ON THE ELEVATOR A FEW MINUTES AGO.

I MUST CONFESS: MY GIVEN NAME WAS JEROME SCHADOU. IN THE THIRD YEAR OF ARCHITECTURE SCHOOL I CHOSE TO CALL MYSELF "SELLADORE" IN LOVING MEMORY OF THOSE HUMBLE BASEMENT PORTALS UPON WHICH WE ALL TREAD.

IT'S NOT AN UNCOMMON NAME.

THE SEXUAL IMAGERY IN MY DREAMS IS UNDERSTANDABLE. I SPEND THE WAKING HOURS OF EACH DAY EXAMINING, FROM A DISTANCE, THE POSTURES AND BODY MOVEMENTS OF A THOUSAND STRANGE WOMEN. WHAT ELSE SHOULD I DREAM OF?

I KNOW OF ONE CAFETERIA THAT'S OPEN ALL NIGHT.

I REFUSE TO BELIEVE THAT YOUR DREAMS WERE THE CAUSE OF MY PROJECT'S FAILURE. BOTH WERE CAUSED BY SOME THIRD, UNKNOWN AGENCY.

BOOM

THE EARTHEN FOUNDATION OF "CARFARE CITY" IS SUDDENLY DEEPENED BY TEN INCHES.